ABOUT THE AUTHOR

Sujit comes from an academic background in Political Science, Law and International Relations. Educated both in Kolkata and London, he was a Civil Servant for 35 years before retiring from the Ministry of Defence. Since then, he is best known as a writer and speaker on many cultural and socio-political issues.

For Bacchu
with all good wishes

Sujanda
25-3-18

'This is a gentle and thoughtful account of a well lived life by one of the earlier migrants from Bengal to London. It is very readable and particularly aimed at family and friends.'

Clare Short, British Politician

'I appreciate fully your autobiography as your unique experience of bridging two cultural experiences and witnessing important events in both Indian and British histroy. All life experience is unique and, therefore, precious and it is our good luck when some part of it is shared with friends or even with unknown people. I am convinced that your book will be well received.'

Dr Imre Bangha, University of Oxford

'I know of many who wanted to write their autobiography and then got stuck. Writing one's first book in an advanced age is a real challenge. It is admirable that you have been able to do it.'

Dr Martin Kampchen Author and Biographer,
Visva-Bharati and Germany

'Congratulations for completing the book. It looks like a very interesting read. It will also be a lovely thing for your children and grand children.'

Dr John stevens, SOAS London

MY JOURNEY FROM AN ASIAN BRITISH TO A BRITISH ASIAN

SUJIT BHATTACHARJEE

Matador
9 Priory Business Park,
Wistow Road, Kibworth Beauchamp,
Leicestershire. LE8 0RX
Tel: 0116 279 2299
Email: books@troubador.co.uk
Web: www.troubador.co.uk/matador
Twitter: @matadorbooks

ISBN 978 1788039 864

British Library Cataloguing in Publication Data.
A catalogue record for this book is available from the British Library.

Printed and bound by CPI Group (UK) Ltd, Croydon, CR0 4YY
Typeset in 11pt Aldine401 BT by Troubador Publishing Ltd, Leicester, UK

Matador is an imprint of Troubador Publishing Ltd

In loving memory of my parents.

CONTENTS

INTRODUCTION

This book is what is commonly called an autobiography. It covers much of my life, from the time I grew up in India, to my life as one of the first-generation Indian immigrants living permanently in the UK; a span of fifty years.

Many books have been written, and much research undertaken on the memories, sufferings, aspirations, fears and hopes of first-generation immigrants or expatriates as they are sometime called. V S Naipaul's *The Enigma of Arrival* tells us about his own emigration from Trinidad to New York, and then to Oxford, and his gradual absorption of the new places. Jhumpa Lahiri's *Interpreter of Maladies* gives an account of the lives of Indian Americans caught between the two cultures. Bharti Mukherjee's *Jasmin* depicts the life of a young woman changing her identity a few times, to be able to adapt to the American way of life. More recently, the New York based author Suketu Mehta, came out with a short book, *What is remembered* on Indo-American Immigrant experience – does living in a new place result in letting go of the past or clinging on to it. So, why another book – and that too from an unknown Indian? This is because although I am part of a long history of Indian immigrants present in Britain, not all experiences of immigrants are the same. We each have our own personal stories to tell.

My experience, like many others of my age, has two phases. Initially, as a person from one country moving to a new one, with the mother country India having the major pull and effect on me – this has gradually faded over the years. I would like to call the first few years of this an Asian British phase. Time passed, life evolved and I adapted to a new and increasingly purposeful life for me to begin with, and then for my family. The close mental tie with the mother country did not evaporate but inevitably became loosened. Gradually, the Asian British in me came to be replaced by a new phase of my life as a British Asian. I began subscribing to the view that one's identity could be multiple and situational. I believe that this twofold experience of my life, initially in India and then in the UK will be of some interest to both my fellow immigrants as well to the general British public. British people's understanding of the trauma and experience of people of Indian origin moving to this country has not been very clear. My hope is that the account of my life in this book will help them to have a better understanding of the identity dilemma of a hybrid immigrant in this country.

After living here for nearly 50 years now, I have witnessed a drastic change in the nature and composition of this country. From a predominantly Anglo-Saxon Christian society it has now become a noticeably diverse and liberal nation. This image is tarnished from time to time by xenophobic reactions to newcomers, but there is no doubt that both Asian immigrants and host nation have gradually created a population in this country, which is largely tolerant and multi-culturally enriched. To some extent, this was inevitable. Advances in transport and communication have made migration easier, giving rise to the currently popular expressions such as dual heritage and multiple identities. I was fortunate to witness this transformation at a time when intolerance to other cultures, religions and races were, and still are, so blatant in many other countries around the world. This is something worth telling.

My own children and grandchildren were always keen to know how and why I came to this country and settled to be the person I have become as a British Indian father and grandfather. My hope is that this autobiography will be a useful legacy to them as second- and third-generation British; growing up within a mixed culture, in which values – Eastern and Western – will always interact in different forms in their lives. As they seek to integrate into British society and culture, they may find valuable and endearing the different phases in the life of an early Diaspora, the long-drawn adjustment process he faced and his lifelong experience.

Finally, in old age, life can end up forlorn and meaningless. After seventy years you become somewhat insignificant and simply dodder around towards the grave. Running a marathon, swimming the Channel or exploring the Antarctic are some of the ways many old people try to keep themselves active and productive. Getting my own life experiences down on paper is my chosen way to give some meaning to the life I have lived. What you gather in life is important but what you scatter tells what kind of life you have lived.

"Writing a book is a horrible exhausting struggle, like a long bout of some painful illness," said George Orwell. Writing one's life story can be even more difficult because memory fades as you grow older and not many have the uncanny ability to recall their lives in full. Relying on memories as far as I can recollect at my age, I have sought to make this book a narrative reliving of my life from the early years to the time of writing this book

I hope my book will be well worth a read.

ACKNOWLEDGEMENTS

There are many people I would thank for helping me with the content, expression and the format of this autobiography. My son Abhik and daughter Suparna were the first to come up with the idea of documenting the memorable events of my life in India and the UK (partially as a way of keeping me busy during my retirement!). Suparna also helped to edit my initial manuscript. My heartfelt thanks go to both.

This book would not have been possible without the constructive support of my wife Gourie. No words can do justice to express my deep gratitude to her for all her help.

I also owe a debt of thanks to many others who knowingly or unknowingly inspired and encouraged me to write this book, including in particular my brother Sudip, sisters Purnima and Sumita and brother-in-law Sibesh. My deepest thanks also go to Dr William Redice for his very helpful suggestions.

Finally, enormous thanks to all those at Matador and Troubador Publishing Ltd, who helped to bring this memoir into fruition.

1

EARLY LIFE IN INDIA

CHILDHOOD IN SILCHAR

I was born in 1939, significantly, the year of the outbreak of the Second World War. I grew up in a town called Silchar in the Indian State of Assam in India. It was originally a part of the Sylhet District during the time of the British East India Company. It was included in Assam by British rulers in 1832 to end the dominance of the Mughal Kings.

Silchar is the headquarters of Cachar District and is the second largest town of the state of Assam in terms of population and area. In colonial days, it was a very peaceful town. The town was aptly named an "Island of Peace" by no other than India's Prime Minister – the late Indira Gandhi. At the time of British rule, many ships were docked for commerce at the bank of its river Barak, which was covered with stones. Many believe that this gave rise to its name "Shil Chor" meaning the Bank of Stones. As time passed, this name presumably got simplified to "Silchar."

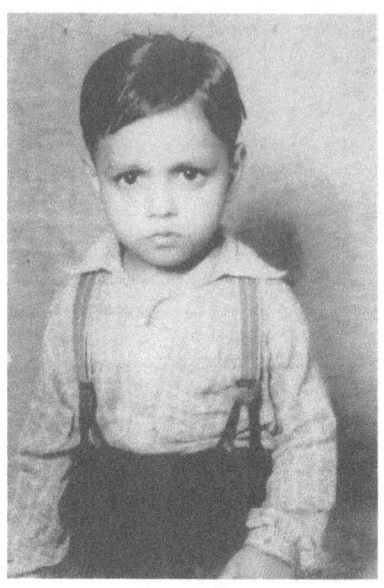

Author, aged 3

Silchar is renowned for the surrounding tea estates, numbering approximately 100, big and small. Many of these are the best scenic spots in Assam. In 1839, British companies began to produce, process, and package what came to be known as Assam tea, noted for its strong and pungent flavour. They found the climate and the soil ideally suited to the production of this high quality tea which was exported to various parts of the world.

I accompanied my father on many occasions on his inspection tours of tea gardens as part of his official duties. One lasting memory that has remained with me was the sight of the tea garden workers, particularly women, picking tea leaves and putting them in baskets on their back, in a scenic and peaceful environment. However, the surroundings were quite eerie at nighttime. I have a vivid recollection of seeing tigers crossing the road with eyes glowing in the pitch-black night while driving through tea gardens at night. Sadly, it was quite common in those days for the tea garden managers to adorn their bungalows with tiger skin rugs, wall mounted deer heads and similar trophies. This, of course, is no longer tolerated and there are now stringent laws against the killing of animals for their skins and to protect our planet's endangered animals.

Silchar has a place in history as a town where some people believe the first polo club in the world was formed in 1859. In the 1850s, British tea planters discovered the game in Manipur on the Burmese border with India. Thereafter, a club was formed and subsequently the first competitive polo match was played in Silchar. A commemorative plaque for this event is located behind the district library.

Silchar, because of its situation by the banks of the river Barak is very often inundated with excessive rainfall and floods in summertime. The situation was worse before the Barak Bridge was built over this river. It was built long after I left Silchar, but I vividly remember Silchar being ravaged by major floods at least on two occasions. The sound and speed with which the water burst into the heart of the town, was really terrifying. For days there was severe damage to households and other calamities resulting from the environmental impact. Stranded residents had to leave their homes and take shelter in makeshift tents on the elevated site of the Polo field, which luckily was too high for flood waters to reach. We too were affected by floods but, because my father was a high ranking government official, were routinely allowed to take refuge in an imposing grand bungalow known as "The Commissioner's Bungalow" situated above the Polo field, so that my father could continue to carry out his official duties.

PARENTAGE

Silchar was the place my grandfather Surjyakumar Torko Saraswati, a renowned Sanskrit scholar, chose as his home. He had a school built in the 1920s for teaching Sanskrit, which earned a good reputation. Our ancestral home was in a well-known place of learning called Panchakhanda in Sylhet, a part of Bengal that went to East Pakistan after partition and is now in Bangladesh. My ancestors are said to have migrated there from Mithila, a famous centre of learning in Bihar. The legend is that one king, Adidharmapa, belonging to the neighbouring kingdom of Tripura, wanted to perform a special religious rite to which he invited and brought some priests from Mithila. Once the rite was performed, five of them were offered five plots of land to settle in his kingdom permanently. These combined plots came to be known as Panchakhondo (meaning "divided in five segments") which became my ancestral home.

My grandfather was an orthodox Brahmin but his children (one daughter and three sons) grew up with ideas that were quite modern for their time. All the sons decided to get a formal school and college education rather than pursue the traditional informal teaching by a priest, which primarily prepared the child for a future as a priest to perform religious ceremonies as a livelihood. I was told by many family members that my grandfather had forebodings of his death. On the day he died, he asked to be laid outside on the veranda. He lay there for a few hours and then passed away after chanting his favourite Sanskrit hymns to Lord Vishnu.

District administration in India is a legacy of the British Raj. My father, Sudhir Bhattacharjee, started his career in government as a Deputy Collector, with responsibility for collecting revenue and some general administration. In the course of duty, he came into contact with many British people who managed various tea estates. He had a high degree of respect for the basic administrative quality of the British. He was also an admirer of various Indian freedom fighters, including Mahatma Gandhi, Sri Aurobindo and Netaji Subhas Chandra Bose. So he must have felt somewhat conflicted in working for our "colonial masters" but never expressed his feelings because the job was important at that time. After India gained independence, he continued to hold many high administrative positions in different places in Assam. It was a matter of great pride for us to discover among his personal documents the following commendation he received from the government of Assam in recognition of his tact and courage in handling a volatile Indo-Pak cross border incident in June 1964:

> *"Government wish to place on record their appreciation of the services rendered by you during the incident in… on the 25th and 26th of June 1964. By your courage, example, devotion to duty and your zeal in the cause of maintenance of peace and order and the protection you afforded to the victims of aggression, you have enhanced your own reputation as an administrator and vindicated Government's pride in having officers like you".*

He was duly elevated to the elite Indian Administrative Service and served for many years as the District Magistrate and Joint Secretary to the government of Assam.

Apart from being a successful administrator, my father was a scholarly person of high intellect and wisdom – well versed in Bengali, English and Sanskrit literature. He was an orator of high repute and the President of the "Shillong Bongo Sahitya Parishad", an august cultural organisation for many years. In recognition of his exemplary administrative experience and great literary knowledge, he was specially selected for the prestigious role of Principal of the Assam Administrative Staff College in Gauhati. That was his last assignment before retirement in 1966.

In contrast to my grandfather (a conservative Hindu Brahmin), my father was truly secular and free from the constraints of traditional religious practices. He also believed in religious freedom. In Silchar, his knowledge of the Koran endeared him to the local Muslim community and he used to receive invitations to speak about Islam during the Eid festival. It would not be out of place to mention here two incidents

My Father

as testimony to his liberal outlook.

When I was eight years old, as a Brahmin, I had to go through a particular religious ceremony called "Upanayan" or thread ceremony. It is a ceremony to initiate a child, in the presence of his family and teachers, to start a second life towards acquiring knowledge and other skills. Normally this ceremony is elaborate and takes a full couple of days, during which time the child remains confined to his own room. It so happened that I had an important Sports Day on the day of the ceremony which I was very keen to attend. When my father came to know about it, initially he was reluctant, but later, and against traditional practice, he relented and gave permission for me to attend this tournament at the end of the ceremony. The ceremony itself was cut short to half a day by the priest at his request.

The second incident happened when my younger sister got married. Many of my friends were invited to come for the wedding and the dinner at the end of the ceremony. I had one Muslim friend among others attending. While there was no problem with the invitation, the sight of my Muslim friend at the communal dinner did not go down well with a few traditional upper-caste Hindu Brahmin guests. This was drawn to the attention of my father, but he didn't give it any importance at all. He called me aside, told me to take good care of my Muslim friend and ensure that he remained unaware of the prejudicial view expressed by a handful of upper caste Brahmins.

My father was the eldest of the three sons and a daughter. Sadly the youngest son died at an early age. My paternal aunt was a formidable lady in total control of her family and home. She was very fond of my father and provided solace and comfort when he needed it most following the sudden death of my mother. The second son, my uncle, Sukumar Bhattacharya, started his career, like my father, as a government official during the Raj and occupied many high positions during his long administrative career. He was more of a pragmatist than my father, and had an imperious presence. But he was also very jovial by nature and loved to tell stories and anecdotes to keep everyone amused. Both my Uncle and Aunt (Amiya) had a very special and warm feeling toward me as the eldest in our family. They had six children, all of whom were dear to me, but the eldest Reena and the youngest Baby have always been the closest. Reena got married to a friend of mine, Arunoday Bhattacharjya, with whom I studied in Kolkata. An Indian Administrative Service Officer by background, Arunoday held many high-ranking positions. Baby's husband, Professor Baladas Ghoshal, is a well-known academic in International Relations. He has written and published widely and is a regular speaker at various international conferences.

After his retirement, my father received a lot of support and companionship from his cousins. One cousin-brother in particular – Bidhu Kaka and his wife, (Kakima) – were frequent visitors to our flat when my father moved to Kolkata. I also fondly remember the many warm and relaxed weekends we spent in their home, with Kakima's wonderful home-cooked sweet dishes – something my father really enjoyed.

My mother's side of the family were settled in a small village called Debipur, close to Rajnagar (aptly named "City of the King") of the Moulvibazar District in Sylhet, now in Bangladesh. It was a peaceful and picturesque place and I have many fond memories of visiting Debipur with my mother in my childhood and enjoying the company of my uncles (Mamas) and aunties (Mashis).

The journey from the nearest rail station to Debipur was both novel and exciting. One had to travel partly by bus, partly by palanquin and the final part by foot. For most of the residents of Debipur and adjacent areas (particularly for women,) the palanquin was a regular mode of transport for both long and short distances. A standard palanquin had space for seating one or two passengers and some were enclosed for protection. They had wooden frames on either side for bearers to carry them. The palanquins were also a common means of transport for carrying brides to the wedding venue. I have a vivid recollection of following on foot the palanquin that carried one of my maternal aunts (Rangamashi) on a bridal chair to her wedding venue some distance away. That was an unforgettable experience. It is now an outdated mode of transport but on the plus side palanquins required no fuel or good roads and did not create pollution.

My maternal grandfather Sarada Charan Bhattacharjee was a well-known headmaster and a respected educator. He owned a large family house with another big house attached to it for members of his joint family. The main house was surrounded by wonderful orchards which had an abundance of bamboo, sugar cane, jackfruit, orange, mango, and lemon trees. My maternal grandmother, Suruchibala Devi (Dadumoni), came from a wealthy aristocratic Zamindar family. She had a very fair complexion and lovely grey eyes. My mother, Debadatta Devi, was the third child among six brothers and sisters.

Visiting Debipur provided me with some wonderful first time experiences. Seeing farmers ploughing the soil in the paddy fields with the help of cattle drawn carts, watching women making food in ovens fuelled with chopped up wood, playing in the rain with splashes of mud all over the body, jumping in the house ponds from the banks, climbing trees and other childhood pastimes will always remain with me in my memories. Unfortunately, the tragic partition of India with Debipur becoming a part of East Pakistan in 1947 brought an end to any further visits. However, two of my maternal uncles (Sisirendu and Subhrendu Bhattachrya) emigrated, and settled to a new and successful life in Kolkata. Sadly, Sisirendu uncle – one of the most gentle, loving and caring person I have ever known – passed away. The other uncle Subhrendu, who is the same age as me, is a retired headmaster, a writer and a well-known literary reviewer.

MOTHER'S UNTIMELY DEATH

I was only eleven years old when my mother died in childbirth on 12th of June 1950. My brother, the youngest one of us four siblings, was only two years old. She died in Shillong, a picturesque hill town in Assam while I, my brother and two sisters were with her on a visit to see Rangamashi, our youngest maternal aunt, Maitreyi, who has always been very close to us.

The night she died in childbirth in Robert Hospital in Shillong still haunts me. It was a dismal and rainy evening; I was at my aunt's house when my father suddenly appeared in a distressed state to fetch me and take me to the hospital. At the hospital I saw my mother lying still in a hospital bed with a white cloth wrapped around her body. I felt something terrible had happened but the impact on me at the age of eleven was more of perplexity than overwhelming sadness. The more I grew up, the more I had the sad realisation in my mind that something enormously precious had gone out of my life and that I would have to live my life without it.

My Mother

My mother was sweet, generous, unassuming and quiet and loved her children enormously. I sadly lost her so early in my life, but my heart is still filled with many beautiful memories of the times we spent as a happy family, her loving embrace, care and affection while looking after us in our childhood. It is said that a good life doesn't come with a manual; it comes with a loving mother. I was very fortunate to have a wonderful mother, and my memories of her are my life's solace and everlasting inspiration.

After my mother died, my father brought us (two brothers and two sisters) up almost singlehandedly, with some assistance from my paternal and maternal aunts. One person who gave us enormous physical and emotional support was Dadumoni. She was a beautiful, generous and very loving person. I can now truly appreciate the trauma she endured to lose her beautiful daughter so young and then find the courage to help raise her grandchildren. She played a key role during my wedding ceremony and was still very alert and lively till she passed away at the age of ninety-two.

Being the eldest of four siblings, I had to take on considerable responsibility. Effectively, I had to become a substitute mother to my younger sisters and brother and carry out some rudimentary day to day childcare activities. I helped with their homework and I even learnt how to do straightforward plaits for girls' hair, to help get my sisters ready for school. Fortunately, we always had reliable, loyal and very good servants who took care of the daily responsibilities of running the house. We were always well nourished, suitably clothed, and often taken out to visit our relatives and acquaintances by our father. He himself was always impeccably dressed and loved to adorn the house with beautiful bits of furniture and *objets d'art*.

My mother with we four siblings

I now realise what my father had to endure to get over his own personal loss and try to balance his extremely busy working life with the life of a widower with four children, including two very young daughters. His life was one of selfless sacrifice for his children. He was only forty-five years old when my mother died and he did not re-marry. Since that time, the quality of courage, strength, duty, responsibility, sacrifice, patience and love that he showed for the rest of his life in order to raise his four children and give them a better life are beyond belief, and we all remain so grateful.

SCHOOLING AND MOVE TO KOLKATA

I finished my schooling at the age of fifteen from Silchar Government School. I was not a brilliant student but always

As a student in Gurucharan College, Silchar (1955)
Standing 4th from the left

had good school reports sent to my father. Mental arithmetic was a subject in which I was not particularly strong, but I remember how some of my more proficient fellow students used to come to my aid. However, I liked doing extra reading beyond school books and, particularly, knowing about historical events. I do not have very many recollections of my teachers, but I remember that I enjoyed the affection of all, including the headmaster, Mohsin Ali, who was a strict disciplinarian.

After completing school, I did my Intermediate from Gurucharan College, one of the premier collegiate institutions in Assam, in 1956. It was a co-educational college, so it gave me my first opportunity to interact with female classmates, intellectually and socially, through joint participation in various activities. Emotional attachments developed naturally but, before they could progress into something more lasting, I moved to Kolkata (then known as Calcutta) for higher education.

Silchar still holds a special place in my heart because of so many wonderful memories of my childhood and adolescent period of my life. I left Silchar almost sixty years ago and, sadly, I was not able to visit the town again although I very much wanted to. From time to time I go there in my mind, but from what I have heard the place has changed beyond recognition over the years.

2

ARRIVAL IN THE HISTORICAL CITY OF KOLKATA

BRIEF HISTORY

Calcutta was renamed to its pre-colonial Bengali name (after the original village of Kalikata) in January 2001. Many believe that the new name has its origin in the Hindu Goddess Kali.

The historical narrative played out over the years is generally that the city of Calcutta was founded by Job Charnock, an agent of the East India Company, in 1690, with the purchase of three villages – Kalikata, Sutanuti, and Govindpur – from a local landlord, Subarna Roy Chaudhury. This claim was challenged in Calcutta's High Court in 2003 by the descendants of the above landlord's family. The Court ruled that no one person could be said to be the founder of Kolkata and that historically, Kolkata had grown over a period of time predating 1690.

An incident in Calcutta on 20th June 1756 (named the "Black Hole of Calcutta") has often been cited in British history as evidence of both Indian Mughal savagery and British stoicism in the face of extreme adversity. It involved the alleged death by suffocation of 123 of the 146 British prisoners held captive on the orders of the Nawab of Bengal, Siraj-ud-daula. According to one of the survivors, John Holwell (who later became the Governor of Bengal), they were held in a room at Fort William which was twenty-four feet wide by eighteen feet long, with one or no windows and no food or water. Subsequent historical findings have questioned the reliability of this report. Many anomalies were found, particularly in terms of the size of the room, the number of windows and the number found dead. Furthermore, the retaliation from the British was no less brutal. Embellished or not, sadly the city of Calcutta was for a time more heavily associated with the Black Hole incident than with its great historical role as a colonial city.

My first impression of Kolkata was one of both awe and beauty when I arrived from Silchar in 1958. To come from a small town to a big city like Kolkata was enormously daunting, but the city soon captivated me with its culture and splendour. I was aware of the western influence in many of Kolkata's architectural monuments but had no idea how deep and varied it was until I saw some of its historical buildings.

Among the city's historical British heritage is the Victoria Memorial, the grand monument that Lord Curzon, the Viceroy of India, built as an imperial proclamation of the mighty force of the rule of Queen Victoria between 1906 and 1921. It was built in the same brilliant Rajasthani stone as the Taj Mahal, to blend classical western influence with Mughal architecture. The Kolkata High Court building, built in neo-Gothic style, was modelled on the 13th century Stand Haus

(Cloth Hall), the medieval commercial building in Ypres, Belgium. Raj Bhavan, the former seat of the Viceroys in India and now the Governor's House, is a replica of Kedleston Hall, an English County House in Derbyshire. The Writers Building, once the East India Company's headquarters, was built in the Gothic style. The Calcutta Museum was built in the Italian style. These are just a few examples that show how the blending of European ideas with Indian tradition helped Kolkata to develop into a major trading, administrative and cultural centre in India's colonial history.

Kolkata was the capital of the British Indian Empire and a major trading, administrative and cultural centre for almost 140 years from 1772 until the capital was moved to Delhi in 1911. Many believe that a growing nationalistic, anti-imperialistic feeling among the local intelligentsia in Kolkata was the reason behind this. According to the historian, Jon Wilson, Delhi *"was the safest place for the imperial state to rule in India in dangerous times"*. After India gained independence in 1947, the state of Bengal was partitioned, with Kolkata remaining in India as the capital city of the state of West Bengal. Initially partition, and later the 1971 Indo-Pakistan war, led to a massive influx of refugees from East Pakistan/Bangladesh into Kolkata resulting in dramatic overpopulation and economic decline. Sadly, the long rule of West Bengal for thirty-four years (1977 to 2011) by the Marxist Communist Party of India (CPM) had no long lasting impact in improving the situation. Since 2011, Kolkata has had a new Government – Trinamool Congress, led by the redoubtable Mamata Banerjee. Opinions are split about the success she has achieved in reinvigorating Kolkata like nobody else – she is largely viewed as a controversial but influential Chief Minister of West Bengal.

ANGLO-INDIAN COMMUNITY

The inhabitants of Kolkata are mainly Bengali but there are many other communities such as the Biharis, Chinese, Nepalese, Marwaris and others who settled in this city over the years. However, there is one particular community whose presence in Kolkata and many other cities like Mumbai, Kochi, Bangalore and Jabalpur has always intrigued me while I was living in Kolkata. They are the Anglo-Indian community, mostly concentrated in the Ripon Street area of Central Kolkata. There was an incorrect perception when I was there about them being entirely pro-British in their attitude and lifestyles, exacerbated by a very sketchy knowledge about their history and contribution.

Anglo-Indians emerged as a mixed race out of the British colonial policy of self-preservation by encouraging British males to marry Indian women. The policy did not last long but the children grew into ethnically diverse Anglo-Indians, not surprisingly more "Anglo" than "Indian". After the independence of India, many Anglo-Indians migrated to Britain, Australia the USA but a substantial number chose to remain in India, and have gradually merged into the mainstream population.

The contribution of the Anglo-Indian community towards the building and maintenance of India's physical infrastructure and particularly in the development of Indian railways has been enormous. As teachers, nurses, doctors, and in sports, secretarial duties and others, they played vital roles in India's nation building.

Some well-known Anglo-Indians – meaning persons of any mixed British and Indian parentage, include the likes of actress Vivien Leigh, actors Boris Karloff, Ben Kingsley, writer Rudyard Kipling, singers Cliff Richard, Engelbert Humperdinck, cricketer Nasser Hussain and many others.

3

HIGHER EDUCATION AND TEACHING

GRADUATION AND HIGHER EDUCATION

After arriving in Kolkata, I sought admission to some of the well-known colleges in Kolkata. I arrived too late to be considered for admission to the renowned Presidency College, but was offered the opportunity to be admitted to its allied college at that time, Central Calcutta College (Old Islamic College) with the privilege of sharing the same hostel facilities at the widely known Eden Hindu Hostel.

Eden Hindu Hostel is a hostel of enormous historical importance. It was established almost 132 years ago and has hosted many notable alumni, including the first President of India, Dr Rajendra Prasad and the Nobel Laureate Economist, Amartya Sen, as boarders. Although I had the option to join two other premium colleges (St Xavier's and Scottish Church), I decided to enlist at the Central Calcutta College and graduated with Honours in Economics and Political Science in 1958.

In 1960, I acquired a Master's degree in Political Science. At the same time I was also doing a part time law course and obtained a Bachelor's degree in Law (LLB) from the University of Kolkata in 1961. The University of Kolkata was founded in 1857 as part of the efforts by a group of British ruling class liberals, to spread western education in India in the nineteenth century. I was then enrolled as an Advocate in Calcutta High Court, the oldest High Court in India that had been established in 1862. Whilst studying law, I was a boarder at another popular hostel – the Hardinge–which was well known as a hunting ground for parents to find their future sons-in-law. I escaped their clutches, but had three wonderful years at this unique hostel, which sadly is no longer in existence. Then, I moved to a flat at the Government Housing Estate in Karaya Road (Park Circus) where I lived for about five years from 1962 to 1967, before I came to London. During these five years, I worked as a Lecturer in Political Science and Commercial Law at Rastraguru Surendranath College, a well-known college in Barrackpore, in North Kolkata.

TEACHING IN BARRACKPORE

Many believe that that the name "Barrackpore" has originated from the English word "barrack "as a cantonment site of the East India Company in 1772. No doubt that it was an important British military and administrate centre. It was also the place where the Indian Mutiny of 1857 started with an attack by an Indian soldier named Mangal Pandey. He was later court-marshalled and hanged.

Rastraguru Surendranath College was a general co-educational degree college in arts and commerce. It was also a hot-bed of politics at that time. Both the ruling Congress party

As a lecturer in Rastraguru Surendranath College, Barrackpore (1962-66)
Sitting fourth from the left

and the leftist Communist party wanted to keep the college within their political control. So when I applied for lectureship at this college, I was fully aware that my appointment was very much dependent on the will of the governing body controlling the college which was pro-Congress, as well as the support of the Teachers Council, which was dominated by left-leaning members. With a careful dose of diplomacy I managed to appease both bodies to get selected. As it was a co-educational college and I was only twenty-three years old, there was some hesitancy to confirm my selection but that too was resolved after an amicable meeting with the chairman of the governing body.

The next five years were the most enjoyable times for me as a teacher. I very soon realised why teaching is considered a noble profession. As a teacher, you come into contact with the most precious resource of human kind – the future generation who are at a tender age and so, idealistic, vulnerable and easy to mould. You help them to learn what you know, but the way you connect with them to inspire and evoke their interest has a greater impact on their learning. Without realising it, you become a role model. That is a huge responsibility to undertake if your commitment is not just to teach, but also to shape, motivate and help students to acquire the skills necessary to have a useful career and take on various challenges in life. A quotation ascribed to Kautilya, an ancient Indian teacher, philosopher and strategist, says it all *"A teacher is never an ordinary person. Construction and destruction can be produced in his lap."*

With hindsight, I think my personality, tact and diplomacy helped make a very positive impact in the mind of the students, principal and other colleagues during my time at the college. Furthermore, as an acknowledgement of my involvement and contribution to a variety of student and teacher-oriented activities, I was given the honour of playing an important double role as the Secretary of the Teachers Council as well as the President of the Students Union. This helped to heal some longstanding disputes between the management and the students union. This was a high point of my tenure at this college.

I left my assignment with the Rastraguru Surendranath College in March 1967.

4

ARRIVAL IN THE UK

ENGLISH WEATHER

It was a rainy and dismal afternoon on the 29th April 1967 when I arrived at Heathrow. My first impression matched the perception I had, like most people in India, about the English weather. It is said that water, wind and wet weather have shaped this island over many millennia. However, very shortly I had to change my views as the whole summer of 1967 turned out to be one of the best on record. Long sunny days with clear bright skies and the sun shining until about nine o'clock at night were an unexpected but most enjoyable experience for me. English weather is, if anything, freakish.

That was the beginning of my deep and sustained liking for a country in which I should have felt alienated on arrival. It did not take too long to adjust because of the companionship and help I was lucky to receive from some of my close friends who were already living in this country. One of them, Tarun Roy, a fellow lecturer from Rastaguru Surendranath College where I worked, was living in a flat in Finsbury Park (a popular residential location for expat Bengalis) with two other friends Adhir Ganguly and Kamalesh Chaudhury. They kindly put me up at their flat on my first night in London and also arranged temporary accommodation for me in a bedsit in Tufnell Park. My acquaintance with Adhir and Kamalesh grew to a lasting friendship but, a few months ago I got the sad news of Tarun's death in Kolkata. Honest and straight talking, I have many good memories of him both in Kolkata and in London.

About the same time, another very close friend of mine, Pinu Shom was sharing a flat in Maida Vale (an affluent part of West London) with two other friends Manthu Das and Deepak Roy. They were happy for me to share their flat in 75 Randolph Avenue, so I moved out from Tufnell Park. I was never lonely in their company, unlike many newcomers who sometimes suffer from depression and loneliness. From then onwards, my life revolved around work and two important sources of enjoyment for any young person – pub-crawling and weekend parties.

PUB CULTURE

The pub as a place for drinking and socialising is fundamental to the culture of this country, and it did not take long for me to appreciate that. There was nothing more enjoyable than having a pint of real ale or lager with friends after a hard day at work. According to a study from the University of Oxford, living close to a pub makes people significantly happier, and the pub – (now known as The Warrington) we regularly visited was very close to our flat. It is regrettable that the pubs are gradually declining – a substantial number close every week. In 1935 there were around 77,500 pubs in the UK, now there are about 50,000. However, there is some revival in the rise of what are called "micro-pubs", which go back to basics. Without loud music and games machines, they tend to be in a single-room communal setting to promote conversation over traditional British ales and stouts. Pubs have no doubt an enormous social value.

FUN-FILLED WEEKENDS

Weekends were a great chance to relax and rejuvenate in many other ways including driving to visit friends and places of interest. I bought my first car – a blue Morris Minor for the princely sum of seventy pounds. Because of the age and price, it had some bodywork defects but the inside was comfortable and the engine most reliable. It is a pity that the production of this car was discontinued and, no wonder, it is now considered a classic, iconic car.

There was a hilarious incident involving this car. Soon after I bought it, I found out that one of the wipers was not working and the bonnet release catches were faulty. I was planning to get these repaired but before I could do so, a friend of mine arranged a blind date for me to meet up with a girl at Victoria station. On the appointed day I drove down to the station, parked the car and was about to go inside when I saw a policeman looking at my car. I looked back and to my horror noticed that I had parked in a place specified for police vehicles only. I ran back and moved the car to a public parking space, but by that time the policeman had sauntered to the front of my car. In a very polite way he started questioning me about the registration, insurance and MOT documents. Unfortunately I was not carrying any these documents and I freely admitted my guilt. I wished the matter to end there

Author in 60s

but it got worse when the policeman asked me to the bonnet. I went through the pretence of opening it but could not open because I knew it was jammed. He then asked me to switch on the wipers and, as I expected, only one worked. During this interrogation, the policeman was writing his notes and I was terrified and prepared for the worst such as a hefty fine, getting points on my licence or even losing it. To my utter delight and amazement the officer simply warned me to be more careful in future, asked me to take all car documents to the nearest police station and get the car repaired within one week's time. I was no doubt very lucky on that occasion, but then the police officers in those days were exceptionally polite and considerate in their dealings with the public.

My ordeal did not end there on that day. Because of my encounter with the police, I was late for my blind date appointment. I went inside the station. The station was crowded. I ran my eyes over the place. I was supposed to meet up with a girl wearing a red dress. I could not see any, but I noticed a girl wearing a black coat with an anxious look waiting in a corner. I approached her and soon found out that she was my blind date. After apologising for my delay I told her that I was looking for a girl wearing a red dress. She said she was wearing one and opened up her black coat to reveal a red dress underneath. We both realised that there was a misunderstanding and laughed at the thought of me going round all the girls waiting in the station and asking them what colour dress they were wearing inside – no doubt I would have been labelled a "creep" or "perv". I took her to a nearby restaurant, conversed for a while and then departed without making any future plan. My blind date fizzled out on this occasion.

Another exciting aspect of my weekends was fun-packed parties – a great way to celebrate an occasion, meet new people and remain in contact with your close friends. Our flat in Randolph Avenue was a well-known venue for holding parties and I always loved to be involved in organising them. While enjoying a party is easy, organising a good one takes a lot of effort in terms of inviting friends, selecting music, setting up the venue, arranging food and drink and more importantly ensuring that nothing goes wrong on the night of the party. Parties were immense source of enjoyment for us as bachelors and more importantly fun ways to provide a social network to overcome loneliness and depression.

5

LONDON LIFE IN THE SWINGING 60S

I was fortunate to be in this country as a young man in the swinging 60s – the era of the Beatles, Stones, Bob Dylan, flower children, hippies, drugs, brightly coloured clothes, bell-bottomed jeans, tie-dyed T-shirts, platform shoes, miniskirts, transcendental meditation, free love, just to name a few of its highlights. *Times* Cartoonist Peter Brooks, who was a London Art student at that time, aptly called it "a truly golden, fabulous time". While I was not quite young enough to play a full part in this new explosion of culture, I immensely savoured the general atmosphere around that time – one of freedom, enjoyment and optimism.

Socially and politically, that was also a period of counterculture and drastic transformation in social norms, as depicted in the American rock musical *Hair* – the story of a group of bohemian hippies and their fight against war and military service. One particular song of that musical "The age of Aquarius Let the sunshine in" epitomized the quest for peace, love, tolerance and freedom, and young people rebelling because they felt something was wrong with the capitalist society in which they were raised. Society and music went together to express a moral outrage that also took the form of students rioting in Paris to assert their rights and several anti-Vietnam war demonstrations. There was a distinct political shift to the left in the UK, the USA and across Western Europe with an ambition to create a more just and egalitarian society. Like many others, I took part in an anti-Vietnam War demonstration in 1968 in front of the American Embassy in London and distinctly remember being moved and elated by the speech of Tariq Ali, the firebrand political campaigner.

Unfortunately, the euphoria of the swinging sixties did not last long. Conservatives have always denounced the decade as one of irresponsible excesses and the decay of social order. While this may be an exaggeration, there is no doubt that many of the social changes that began in the sixties were not carried out to their full course or universally accepted. This was shown clearly through one of the main characters in *Hair*, Claude. He was torn between freedom and the reality of the surroundings that challenged him.

As a result, the sixties came to be viewed largely as a reaction to the War and Victorian values. Living in communes away from the real world provided joy and serenity for a while but once faced with the reality of a more practical, selfish and commercial world, the young failed to deal with it properly. Marianne Faithful, a leading symbol of the sixties, herself said in an interview *"It was a big problem for me in the sixties, especially as I had to pretend everything was so wonderful, wild and sexual."* One big problem was that many young people got horribly addicted to the drugs they experimented with and died young. At a time when some of my friends and colleagues were experimenting with cannabis and LSD, I was comparatively weak-minded and too frightened of their long-term consequences and so, I never let myself experience any form of drugs.

However, more than anything else, the 60s were certainly happier times as life appeared simpler, less complicated and incredibly free. There was greater trust, respect and neighbourliness. The era gave an impulse to expose many deceptions of the current age. It was also a better time to have been a student with student grants and no shortage of work. The music was most enjoyable with the Beatles, John Lennon particularly, the Rolling Stones, the Who and Pink Floyd all in their prime. However, if the music you love tells you about your own personality, my liking was more for soft, gentler, melodious romantic forms of music as well as songs of protest and social justice rather than rock, and heavy metal. Among the solo artists, whose songs will always remain in my heart were Petula Clark's *This is my Song,* Engelbert Humperdinck's *Release Me,* Joan Baez's *We shall Overcome,* Neil Diamond's *Sweet Caroline,* Bob Dylan's *Blowing In The Wind,* Louis Armstrong's *What a Wonderful World,* Elvis Presley's *Love me Tender* and Frank Sinatra's *I Did it My Way.* It was quite common at that time, for most of the weekend parties to conclude with Engelbert's *The Last Waltz.* So, in spite of many excesses, the era was one of the most fun-filled and exciting decade's people will ever see.

The Victoria and Albert Museum recently ran an exhibition called *"You Say You Want a Revolution? Records and Rebels 1966-1970".* I did not see it but I understand that it provided a wonderful nostalgic trip down the memory lane of the swinging 60s through light shows and fashion screens. According to Victoria Broackes, the senior curator, the objective was to initiate a debate about an era which she considered was "the best of times and worst of times".

6

FURTHER EDUCATION IN THE UK

My initial life in London was not all fun and pleasure. There was a great deal of uncertainty and anxiety about both study and work. Before coming to this country, I was planning to go to the USA to do a PhD in International Relations at the University of Pennsylvania. That did not materialise because of the foreign exchange restrictions in operation at the time. I was advised to get a job voucher to come to the UK to work for a while and then try to go to the States for further study as another option. This option was attractive to me for another reason. At about the same time, I was lucky to be accepted by Lincolns Inn to pursue my career in law as a barrister. I therefore decided to apply for the job voucher, got it within couple of months, and arrived with it in the United Kingdom in April 1967.

After arriving, there was a sudden change in plans about which I still have some regrets. Historically, a call to the Bar in this country involved both part-time studies and attendance of some social events (including dinners at the Inns of Court) with other members of the profession. Unfortunately, the system changed by the time I arrived. The new requirement was for all student barristers to undertake a one year full-time professional course followed by a year of pupillage while remaining self-employed. I realised that to do a full-time course would be very expensive for me. I could have written to my father asking for help but decided against it. Another factor was the possibility that I might return to India at some stage to practice law as I was already an advocate enrolled at the Kolkata High Court.

So, instead of spending a lot of money on a course that I considered not strictly necessary, and in order to earn a living, which of course was necessary, I joined the British Civil Service. Within a year or so, I was fortunate to be given an opportunity of unpaid leave to undertake a year-long Master of Science (MSc) degree course in International Relations at the University College London. I completed that course with the primary objective of getting an administrative job with the UNO (United Nations Organisation). Unfortunately I was unaware that there was a quota system in operation at that time which gave preferential treatment to nationals from the newly emerging independent countries. So after obtaining my MSc degree, I re-joined the Civil Service, albeit at a higher grade.

7

WORKING IN THE BRITISH CIVIL SERVICE

As mentioned earlier, my father was a civil servant in India during the colonial days. Although I did not follow in his footsteps, I had some idea about the origin and operation of the civil service – both in colonial days and in the post-independence period.

One of the key individuals involved in the evolution of the Indian Civil Service was Lord Macaulay who served on the Supreme Council of India between 1834 and 1838. His passionate belief, expressed in his 1835 *Minute on Indian Education*, was the need "*to form a class who may be interpreters between us and the millions whom we govern; a class of persons, Indians in blood and colour, but English in taste, in opinions, in morals, and in intellect.*" However, the seed was sown long before that in 1806 when a training establishment called the East India College was built at Haileybury near London to train the administrators of the East India Company. This place is quite close to where I currently live. So I was quite intrigued to know that from 1806 to 1857, the East India Company operated from Haileybury to educate thousands of British civil servants to work in India.

In 1858, the company was wound up but Haileybury and the Imperial Service College continued with this rich legacy to serve the British Empire in India from 1862.

The British civil service, as we know it today, was formed to implement the recommendations in the Northcote – Trevelyan report of 1853. The report foresaw a civil service structure with full-time salaried officers, systematically recruited with clear lines of authority and uniform service rules. Since then the civil service has undergone several radical changes resulting in what it is today – a slim-line structure with ongoing outsourcing of vital government functions.

From 1967, I worked in several civil service Ministries, including the Charity Commission, the Department of Health and the Ministry of Defence. I formally retired as a Senior Management Accountant from the Ministry of Defence in 1999.

Once I started working in the British civil service, I was astonished to find how, when compared to what I had seen in India, it had modernised itself in terms of its ethos. The working environment was informal but still very task-oriented. There was more social interaction and mixing among the staff throughout the 60s, 70s and early 80s before the desktop computer made its appearance. Grade distinctions at different levels were minimal. People were mostly on first-name terms. I distinctly remember attending an office meeting in my first year and my astonishment to find the head of the office sitting alongside one of the office messengers and both talking amiably to each other. I couldn't visualise this happening in India. This is not to say that an instance like this or the discarding of a few outmoded customs has made Britain classless. The divide between the upper class and the rest of the population was and still is as wide as ever. It is just that common people were better off compared to any time previously and appeared not too concerned about the privileges enjoyed by the upper class. The situation has, of course, changed recently with the common people trying to make their voices heard more than ever.

My career as a civil servant did not come easy. I had to work hard for success every step of the way. I was always conscious of the fact that I was an immigrant, and should learn and develop quickly the skills required to do my job. I had invaluable help and guidance from some of my British colleagues at the formative stage. Some are no longer alive but I will remember them with enormous gratitude.

In this connection, one particular touching incident springs to my mind concerning a female colleague who used to sit next to me. She was extremely kind, encouraging and supportive to me throughout the initial stage of my career. One Monday after arriving in office, I found her seat empty. Very soon I found out that she had passed away at the weekend. This came as a great shock to me, but I was more saddened and astonished to see all my other colleagues going about their business as normal. In India, the death of a colleague would normally stop all work in the office and everyone would be talking about him or her for days – so this was a culture shock to me. This was also my first encounter with the stoicism of the British national persona – it is less prone to outward emotional displays with the belief that "life must go on". Following the Times Journalist Richard Morrison, *"the British are the way they are because our climate is damp, dour and undemonstrative."* Probably there is some truth in it.

There were many lessons I learnt from my work and experience in the civil service. One significant lesson learnt was when I was assigned to do an important finance job. Finance was not my forte in my early days and I was naturally nervous about my new job. A junior member of staff – a middle aged lady – was assigned to work for me but very soon I noticed that she was ignoring me and taking all her finished work directly to the head of the branch (who happened to be my immediate boss), seeking his advice on matters about which she should have first consulted me. One of the reasons she had free access to my boss, was because she and the wife of the branch head were good friends. I decided to take my time to learn about my new job as thoroughly as I could. This took about a month. After this, and feeling sufficiently confident, I invited her to have a chat. I told her clearly and firmly that her finished work should be channelled through me for my approval before it was sent to anyone else – including the head of our branch. She wasn't too happy about it and as I expected, complained to my boss. However, my boss was wise enough to know that I had acted correctly and advised her to follow what I had told her to do. The lesson learnt was that if you know your job well and are confident, you will always get recognition and respect irrespective of your background.

Civil servants, in general, were not highly paid, but always enjoyed a good reputation as highly dedicated public servants and were politically neutral. Sadly, certain parts of the British media have always held a deep antipathy towards civil servants and drive their populist agenda by characterising civil servants as *"overpaid, lazy and prone to sickness"* because of their relative job security and inflation-proof pensions. Civil servants earn less than people in the private sector, and are certainly not the only group of workers to benefit from such pensions. This antipathy intensified, for political reasons, once Margaret Thatcher came to power in 1979. Sadly, what I witnessed at the later phases of my career was a planned and systemic ideologically-based attack on the civil service. This led to a ruthless diminution of the size and role of civil servants and the gradual privatisation of government functions as a panacea for social and economic progress. There was a massive devaluation of decision-making power as it was transferred to executive agencies, leading to a fragmentation of the civil service and the ascendancy of political advisers to ministers who have more influence than most civil servants. There was also a misguided belief that efficiency in the public sector could only be achieved by adopting methods and practices of the private sector.

"*The idea of public service is not the same as the motive to maximise profits*", said Adam Smith a long time ago. Baron Robin Butler, head of the civil service from 1988 to 1998, once said "*The idea of the civil service as a comfortable and secure sinecure at the end of it has gone. But it would be folly to replace it with another unsavoury image in which only the bottom line matters and the means of achieving it are a matter of less concern.*" The fundamental principle of accountability to Parliament is never present in the private sector, nor is political impartiality and the ethical code to which civil servants must always adhere.

8

MARRIAGE AND FAMILY LIFE

UNEXPECTED MEETING WITH MY FUTURE WIFE

I had always been an idealistic and romantic type of person. Not surprisingly, I had a few crushes on girls during my schooldays in Silchar as well as in Kolkata during my college/university days. They simply matured into harmless friendships and not to any lasting commitment.

During my time as a happy and fun-loving bachelor in the 60s and 70s in London, I also met many girls with whom friendships were formed – some close, some not that close. Romantic relationships took place which could have been lasting. But there was something in my nature that did not wholeheartedly commend their full bloom. Ralph Waldo Emerson, an eminent author said *"Do not go where the path may lead, go instead where there is no path, and leave a trail."* Some of the girls I met have left a trail of fond memories in my mind.

My life took an unexpected and inexplicable turn in 1975.

During one of my many trips to India, I was visiting the city of Allahabad to meet up with one of my sisters, Sumita, and her husband, Sibesh. Allahabad is a very old and ancient city which hosts the Kumbha Mela, the largest religious gathering in the world. I was thirty-six years old at that time and had already lived for eight years in the UK without settling down. So, there was some family pressure to see me getting married either in England or in India. I was more inclined to marry in England at some stage and not in India, but there is a saying *"Man proposes and God disposes"*.

Once I arrived in Allahabad, I found out that, without my knowledge, my sister had arranged a chance meeting with a well-known family settled in the central Indian city of Jabalpur which was a Cantonment town with many important military establishments. The city is famous for its many popular tourist attractions including Marble Rocks with its spectacular waterfalls and the Kanha Nature Reserve. At that meeting, I met my future wife, Gourie, who (impressively and unusually) was a practising criminal lawyer at that time. The meeting was not that long but there was something in her demeanour that attracted me. Also, I found her legal practice very appealing because of my own legal background. This eventually led to several meetings, then mutual closeness, and an agreement on both sides to get married. It was no doubt a gamble on my part as well as hers, as it was not a so-called "love marriage" with a long courtship. However, as time progressed, we discovered that we had a lot in common, fell deeply in love and became very close. I know now for sure that my gamble was handsomely successful. I was immensely happy to get married to someone who gave me, and has continued to give me, an extraordinary amount joy and satisfaction in my life. Also, I was lucky to find a large, caring, close knit family of in-laws with Gourie's loving mother and charming six sisters and one brother. Sadly, my mother-in-law who we all called 'Bouma' died about two years ago after a being bedridden for about four years following a hip operation. A strong and very lovable person, Bouma was always there in every step of our life and we all miss her very much.

My wife's family is now spread across the world in several countries but, thanks to the internet and ease of travel, we have become a large and loving global family meeting up quite often.

I mentioned the role my sister and brother-in-law played in connection with my marriage. There is no doubt that without their skilful planning, my chance meeting with Gourie would not have taken place. At the time I was ambivalent, but now I know how grateful I am for what they did.

My sister, Sumita Bhattacharya, is a journalist, author and translator with many praiseworthy publications to her credit. She is currently translating the Vedic Scholar Anirban's "*Veda Mimamsa*" from Bengali to English. My brother-in-law Sibesh Bhattacharya is a former head of the Department of Ancient History at the Allahabad University. He was also a British Council Scholar at the School of Oriental & African Studies in London for two years. Before retirement, he served as the Acting Director of the Indian Institute of Advanced Study which is a renowned research centre in Shimla, North India. He held this most prestigious post for more than a year, Shimla is at the foot of the Himalayas and was designated as the cooler summer capital during the British Raj. The Institute is now housed in what was called the Vice Regal Lodge in colonial times.

It was during Sibesh's tenure at this Institute that my wife and I were fortunate to be shown round the innermost part of this majestic building. Located at the top of Observatory Hill of Shimla, it was formerly the residence of the British Viceroy in India. Many historical events took place at this venue and many important documents are preserved in this building. The Shimla Conference between Viceroy Lord Wavell and the Indian political leaders for Indian self-government was held here in 1945. The decision to partition India was also taken here in 1947. After independence, the government decided to make it available for academic use and, since October 1965, the Institute of Advanced Study started functioning from there. It was a rare privilege for us to have a close sight of this historical building and I cannot thank my brother-in-law enough for making it possible.

LOVE AND ARRANGED MARRIAGE

The experience of my own marriage opens up an important issue with which many are familiar – the on-going debate about love and arranged marriages. It is said that in a love marriage, the couple goes through two separate phases – a pre-wedding courtship period, often with both living together, followed by a post-wedding period of a married life. In a negotiated marriage there is technically just one phase – the post-wedding arranged marriage phase. The general assumption is that, happiness in the courtship stage before a love marriage is a sure guarantee for post-wedding happiness. Experience shows that it is not always so. Often the post-wedding phase becomes more critical with the couple gradually discovering many personal weaknesses which do not surface because of the need to keep each other attracted and committed during the courtship stage. This phase needs an on-going effort to share – both joy and pain – and overcome all adversities to stay together as a happily married couple. This does not, in my view, receive as much priority as in an arranged marriage.

On the other hand, there are several instances of people being forced into arranged marriages although they do not like each other, and nothing can be worse than that. As I see it, you can be lucky or unlucky in both love and arranged marriage. What is really important for any couple is to continue to keep each other attracted and bound by mutual love, trust and support throughout their lives.

An arranged marriage, where we had a choice, is very much part of the culture in which we both were brought up. This is therefore very different to what the media in the Western world often highlights, which are in fact 'forced' marriages. In these cases, the girls involved have no say and are often coerced into a marriage.

9

DEATH OF MY FATHER

I lost my father a couple of months after the marriage of my younger brother. The year was 1977, and by then I was a well-settled married man with a loving wife and expecting our first child. Unfortunately, my father did not live to see his first grandchild. His death was a deep shock to me, my brother and two sisters. After he died we found two lines scribbled in his diary: "*I go while the going is good.*"

Among his many sentimental legacies I found a shawl that he often used to wear around the house. This shawl is still with me after many years and I carry it with me each time I visit India because that way his memories of fortitude and self-control live forever with me and continue to give me hope and inspiration

I have always had a guilty and helpless feeling about not being able to do much about my family who today remain in India, particularly at the time when my father was becoming weak and frail due to age. I was so lucky that my brother, Sudip, and sister, Purnima, willingly took on the responsibility to look after him with selfless love and dedicated care for a long time. This continued until my father died. Sadly, several years after that Purnima also lost her husband Taraprasanna, which left a huge hole in her life. Tara's death was devastating for all of us and we have treasured memories of him as being always loving and thoughtful towards his wife. Unfortunately, Purnima has in recent years also started having some health and mobility problems, which restricted her ability to manage on her own. Sudip with the rock solid support of his wife Ambalika have continued to be the selfless carers for Purima over the years.

Sudip is an ex-banker and a prolific writer with many publications on socio-political issues. His book, *Over the years: A Compilation of my Commentaries on Contemporary Issues,* has received high praise. I take pride in his success as a writer and equally in how he and Ambalika have always worked together to take care of Purnima as well as bringing up two wonderful sons – Shomik and Shayon. Both are now happily married and have very successful careers. Shomik's wife Radhika is a high ranking banker and they have recently become parents of a beautiful daughter Tarini. Shayon lives in San Francisco and his wife Devaki is an IT consultant.

10

BRINGING UP CHILDREN

MANAGING WORK AND FAMILY LIFE

After our children (a boy and a girl) were born we had a difficult choice to make about both continuing to remain full-time working parents. With no close family in England to support us, we had difficulty managing financially, having also just bought our first home. At the time, being a full-time working mother was not very common. Employer's attitudes as well as the law in the 70s/80s were not very tolerant of working families. Then we did not have long, paid maternity leave, or flexible paternity leave – which in recent years have enables fathers to help with childcare. Furthermore, flexible working hours, computerised access enabling working from home and a more family supportive working environment, are all major factors in helping families to manage work and family life nowadays. We were extremely lucky to find a wonderful childminder – Mrs Ethrington, who lived with her husband and granddaughter very close to our home.

In fact they became known as 'Nana' and 'Grandad' to our children, and remained a part of our children's' lives until Mr and Mrs Ethrington passed away in the 1990s. Their valuable affectionate advice and guidance enabled Gourie to go back to work after a fairly short maternity leave (3 months) for both children. They were truly like our parents and taught us so much as inexperienced parents. We only had Dr Spock's book to guide us rather than Google and Mums net!

CHOICE OF EDUCATION

One of the major problems we faced at the time was the future education of our children. We were conscious of the fact that, as second-generation Indians in Britain, they would need the best possible education to compete and be successful in their careers. However, our search for a good local school for our son at the age of five resulted in frustration, as we couldn't find one we considered suitable for their needs and our particular circumstances as working parents.

Our children were born at a time when the unfairness of the selective system of schooling led the Labour Government to replace it by a more informal child friendly progressive type of primary and secondary comprehensive school system. The intention was noble in its aim to offer the equal educational opportunities to every child as an entitlement and not a privilege. However, the implementation of the comprehensive system was chaotic and patchy. Furthermore, given the different types of neighbourhoods in which the schools were situated, the change resulted in huge variations in standards between comprehensive schools. The Conservative Government tried its best to thwart its smooth running for political reasons, and the problem was exacerbated by the slackening of standards and discipline in many schools across inner city areas. Both my wife and I had an old-fashioned educational background, in the sense that it was largely based on discipline and respect for the teachers in doing their duties. We tried not to be hyper-demanding parents as advocated by Amu Chua and her husband, Jed Rubenfeld, in their controversial book *The Triple Package*. However, the idea of obedience and keeping a hierarchical difference with the children came naturally to us. So, at a time in the early 80s, when the discipline in schools was becoming an increasingly serious problem, somewhat against our wishes, we opted for private education for both our children. This had the additional advantage that extra-curricular activities such as music, swimming and sports were included in the curriculum. Unfortunately, this involved a longer day at school for them sometimes, but made it easier for us to collect them at a more convenient time after work. Timely collection from school was a problem for us as working parents and still is an issue facing many parents now.

Private versus state education has been and still is a controversial issue. But I believe that parents are entitled to make their own choices for the good of their children. In any case, opting for private schooling was not an easy choice for us, as we both knew that it would be really tough for us to meet the high costs involved. Once we made our choice, the result was years of struggle and sacrifice for both of us. However, we have had no regrets at any stage, as our efforts paid dividends in giving our son, Abhik, and daughter, Suparna, a good foundation for their future careers as a doctor and a commercial solicitor respectively. Maybe having a working mother as an example made them better people in the long run.

MIXED CULTURE

Raising a family in a society that has different norms and values to the one in which we were brought up, has its own inherent challenges. Though this is not unique to immigrant families, it has a long-term impact on the children in particular. I have discussed this under the heading "Inter-generational gap" in the latter part of this book. As Indian parents, our instinct was to be over-protective – especially of our daughter! However, we realised that it was important to nurture the Western value of independence in our children growing up in this society. Whilst we stressed the importance of degrees and qualifications, we tried to encourage them to explore other interests as well.

Both our children enjoyed travelling from an early age. Abhik travelled to Toulouse on his own aged ten, visited India alone during his gap year and went to Australia to play rugby on a school trip. He is currently a consultant anaesthetist in the NHS. He is happily married to an oncologist, Saoirse Dolly, currently working at the Royal Marsden Hospital. In spite of gruelling working hours they are both managing to bring up two wonderful children – their son Arlen and daughter Seren. For us as full time working parents, I think we missed out a lot on having fun with our own children. Weekends and evenings were taken up with catching up on domestic duties and the English weather did not help! Now the best thing that has happened to us is having grandchildren and being a part of their lives.

Our daughter Suparna spent a year at the University of Poitiers in France on an Erasmus Exchange as part of her undergraduate law degree at Cambridge University. Having acquired a taste for French life, she later spent some time working in Paris. She is currently a senior lawyer for a well-known City law firm, specialising in Media, Communications & Technology.

We are enormously proud of all their achievements.

11

MY SON'S WEDDING

I believe that extended families help us grow as individuals, but new relationships add to that dimension enormously. We were delighted when Abhik and Saoirse decided to get married in 2012. Indian weddings are very important family occasions, and so the "Asian" in me wanted to ensure that our families were included in the celebrations. We have a global family now, and due to difficulties of them getting UK visas, as well as age and health factors, we decided to have a Hindu wedding ceremony in Goa. Saoirse's family, including her parents – Professor Oliver Dolly (an eminent scientist and molecular neurobiologist) and his lovely wife, Sheelagh, a former nurse, her sister, Aisling, and some of her extended family were able to attend. My maternal aunt, Rangamashi, who was in her seventies, all our brothers and sisters as well as most of their families were also there. It was wonderful for families from across the globe – India, Dublin, Holland, New York, San Francisco, Hong Kong, Montreal and London to get to know each other and enjoy a really joyous family celebration.

Irish and Indian families have a lot in common in terms of family ties. After Goa, there was another wonderful traditional

Irish celebration in the beautiful 800-year-old Cloghan Castle located in Loughrea, some fifteen miles from Galway in Ireland. This was also a happy and fun event where we met the rest of Saoirse's relatives and friends. The warmth and affection we experienced there made us feel that we had truly "extended" our family.

We also had a reception in London for the many friends who could not make it to either of the non-UK events!

Indeed 2012 was an exhilarating and memorable spring for our family.

12

SOME MAJOR WORKING LIFE EXPERIENCES

Looking back, I can remember many wonderful events taking place over the last thirty-three years of my working life. I recall a few experiences which will always stay in my mind.

SECURE MENTAL HOSPITALS

The first was during the years 1983–1987. I was working in the Mental Health division of the Department of Health. I was part of a team with responsibility for the financial management of the four secure mental hospitals – Broadmoor in Berkshire, Rampton in Nottinghamshire, Park Lane, now called Ashworth in Merseyside and Carstair in Scotland. It is well known that the patients detained in these hospitals were held under high security as most were highly dangerous and posed a grave danger to the public. Some notable patients detained in Broadmoor were the Kray Brothers and more famously Peter Sutcliffe – the Yorkshire Ripper. Ian Brady, one of the Moors Murderers was one of the infamous inmates at Rampton. As part of my job, I had the privilege of visiting these hospitals a few times. In all these hospitals, my other colleagues and I had to go through various levels of security and were escorted by trained nurses to visit different wards before being allowed to meet some of the patients. There was strict surveillance throughout, but the experience was terrifying knowing that most were of dangerous, violent and criminal propensities, and had been convicted of heinous crimes. However, various reforms to mental health were taking shape at that time to improve the conditions and treatments available in these hospitals. As a result, I was able to see a much more open environment and a friendlier form of patient care in operation.

CONVENTIONAL WEAPONS TESTING CENTRES

The second memorable experience was one during my time with the Ministry of Defence (MOD). I was never in the Army nor had any army-related experience. Yet, by a significant twist in my career, I worked for about five years (from 1991 to 1995), for an important weapons testing branch of the MOD– Defence Test & Evaluation Organisation (DTEU), later The Defence Evaluation and Research Agency (DERA). My job was the financial management of four important establishments for testing conventional weapons for the Armed Forces. They were the three land ranges at Shoeburyness in Southend-on-Sea, Pendine in Wales and Eskmeale in Cumbria, the surface-to-air missile range at Aberporth in Wales and the armoured vehicle testing centre at Chertsey in Surrey. They have had significant roles over the years in the development and testing of a variety of military weapons. For someone who had never had any military training and experience, seeing first-hand the intense remotely controlled testing of gunfire and explosions from concrete bunkers was as much informative as scary and mind-boggling.

EQUAL OPPORTUNITIES POLICIES

The third one I remember took place during my time with the Ministry of Defence (MOD). One particular area, in which I got involved, beyond my normal line of duty, was in the ministry's approach to improving the number and status of civilian ethnic minority staff, particularly at higher grades. The MOD's public image was generally very secretive and unsympathetic towards ethnic minority staff. A high-level Steering Committee was formed in 1991 at the behest of the Permanent Secretary to advise and implement the MOD's equal opportunities policies in this respect. I was asked to be a member of that committee and subsequently spent almost eight years helping initiate and implement many of these policies. They included setting targets for recruitment, analysing appraisals and promotion reports, providing equal opportunity-related training and holding personnel at all levels accountable for carrying them out. The progress in this respect was slow, but from 1992 onwards, there was a distinct improvement in developing a workforce to reflect the diversity of British society. It was gratifying for me to get a letter from the Permanent Secretary recognising the important role I played as a member of the aforesaid committee.

Disappointingly, a recent Government study has shown that despite strong commitment from senior management, Whitehall has still got a poor record on diversity – only four per cent of the top 4000 senior civil servants are from an ethnic-minority background. Sir Jeremy Heywood, the cabinet secretary once made a statement *"The civil service takes pride in its differences and we have a duty to become even more representative of modern Britain.*" I hope that the civil service's higher echelons take this pledge seriously and take measures to ensure that the civil service positively reflects the diversity of its workforce.

Here I should emphasise that my involvement within the MOD was with the civilian side of equal opportunity policies only, and not the military. Successive governments have sought to make the army conform to equal opportunities legislation like the civilians and, as a result, there was a slow but much needed cultural change within the armed forces. However, there is a view that the army's main role as a fighting power is likely to get compromised if it aims to be politically correct. General Lord Dannatt, retired Chief of the General Staff, wrote a book recently *Boots on the Ground – Britain and her Army since 1945* which is a very useful analysis of this dilemma. It is worth quoting a relevant observation he has made in that book: "*The army may wish to have a right to be different but it cannot march out of step indefinitely from the society from which its soldiers are drawn.*"

MY RETIREMENT PARTY

The fourth one I remember with fondness was my retirement party. The farewell venue was the Ministry of Defence's renowned Henry VIII's wine cellar within the main building in Whitehall. The event took place in the presence of the Surgeon General who gave a very warm and touching farewell speech.

One normally needs special permission to visit this historical place located deep underneath the ground floor of the main building. It was built in the 1500s by Cardinal Wolsey, which is the reason why it is also called Cardinal Wolsey's cellar. One has to go through some narrow back staircases to reach this Gothic-style stone and brick built place of unique architectural appearance and style. It was a great way to send me off and I felt really honoured to finish my working life on such a high note.

MOD RECORD REVIEW

My final memorable experience began after I formally retired in 1999. I was fortunate to be offered re-employment on a part-time basis for a coveted job within a specialist group of Record Review Officers for the Ministry of Defence. As a Departmental Record Review Officers, we were responsible for reviewing MOD records of files and documents to identify

Farewell on retirement by the Surgeon General (MOD) (1999)

Author with other MOD Record Review Officers (1999-05)

those worthy of preservation (either short- or long-term), or authorise destruction if they were no longer of value to the Department or oversee transfer to the National Archives. It was a highly responsible assignment in the management of information which gave me an opportunity to broaden my knowledge of the Department but more importantly to look at and evaluate many sensitive records in a way that very few people would have access to. This was an exceptional experience in my career.

13

SOME MEMORABLE BRITISH EVENTS AND PLACES

My work with the Ministry of Defence provided me with some wonderful opportunities to visit or be invited to attend some memorable events.

BATTLE OF BRITAIN BUNKER

My first abiding memory of such a visit was looking round the Battle of Britain underground bunker at RAF Uxbridge. The operation room within this bunker is aptly called the "Battle of Britain Bunker" as it is the place which saved Britain during World War II. It took my colleagues and I quite a while to find it, as the bunker is hidden within a dilapidated building under a housing estate. Once inside we had to go down several flights of stairs to find the famous Fighter Command No 11's Operation Room, from where the planning and coordination of the air defence against the

Germans were carried out. As visitors from the MOD, we were fortunate to be allowed to simulate the Battle of Britain, 15th of September 1940, scenario on the plotting table by moving little numbered markers with wooden poles, which were actually used to find out vital information including the location of enemy aircraft, friendly aircraft formation and the weather conditions on the day. The operation room was closed in 1948 but has now been restored as a museum which has a large number of important exhibits in glass cases. The visit was an exceptional historical experience for all of us.

ST JAMES'S PALACE RECEPTION

A second memorable event was attending His Royal Highness the Prince of Wales' reception at St James's Palace State Apartments, on 13th June 1997. St James's Palace is the official residence of several members of the royal family and is also used to host official receptions. I was pleased when I came to know that the Second Round Table Conference relating to India's independence was also held at St James's Palace in 1931.

The reception was arranged to mark the fiftieth anniversary of the independence of India and Pakistan. The idea was to acknowledge the contributions made by some chosen individuals of South Asian origin to life in UK. I was fortunate to be invited among this handful of people for my role and contribution as a member of the MOD's Ethnic Minority Steering Committee in taking forward its equality policies. The reception gave me an opportunity to meet the Prince of Wales and many other dignitaries present for the occasion. The meeting with the Prince of Wales was brief but very pleasant. I was impressed by his deep knowledge and interest in India.

TROOPING THE COLOUR

The third memorable event that springs to mind is attending the Queen's Birthday Parade known as Trooping the Colour. This is traditionally held in June every year on Horse Guards Parade, Whitehall, with a military parade and march-past of real pomp and grandeur. The event has its origin in the early eighteenth century. The Queen's colour of a battalion of foot guards is "trooped"; they march slowly with their flags between the soldier's ranks, before the Sovereign. I was lucky to receive free passes from the MOD to the seated stands from where my wife and I could watch the whole spectacle of assembled regiments with the Queen receiving a salute from the saluting base.

THE QUEEN MOTHER LYING IN STATE

The fourth event which stands out is when I was invited to pay respect to Queen Elizabeth, the Queen Mother who died on 30th March 2002. As is the tradition with Kings and their consorts, the Queen Mother's body lay in State for three days in Westminster Hall before her funeral on 9th April 2002. Westminster Hall is the oldest building in Parliament and almost the only part of the ancient Palace of Westminster which survives in almost its original form. The Hall was built in 1097 under William II (Rufus), the son of William the Conqueror, and was completed two years later. I was able to visit Westminster Hall on the second day and was very much moved by the solemnity surrounding the occasion.

PALACE GARDEN PARTY

Another notable event that I treasure was attending a garden

My family at The Queen's Garden Party 1998

party at Buckingham Palace on 9th July 1998. This event is held three times a year. The first Royal Garden Party was held during the reign of Queen Victoria. These parties are held to welcome a cross-section of the British public for their various contributions towards society. I was, therefore, immensely delighted to receive the official invitation from the Lord Chamberlain for me and my family.

The day of the event turned out to be very warm and sunny. My son and I were wearing lounge suits, my wife a sari and my daughter a formal dress. We entered through the Buckingham Palace gates and were directed to pass through the palace to get into the lovely looking garden. That was the beginning of an unforgettable afternoon for us. The lawn was teeming with people wearing morning/lounge suits, tails, top hats, military uniforms and national dress of different sorts to present a colourful spectacle. But the general ambience was relaxed and informal. Before the Queen arrived, we had the traditional English treat of tasteful cucumber sandwiches, scones and cakes with tea. The Queen entered the garden accompanied by a military brass band. She and other members of the royal family circulated through specially selected people. We did not meet the Queen face to face – most people generally do not – but we had the chance to see her up very close as she walked passed us.

It was such an extraordinary day overall for me and my family but there was more to it for me to remember the big day. As we were returning from the Palace, we came face to face with a reporter from the *Sunday Mirror* who interviewed me about my experience of attending the Royal Garden Party and about our outfits. This interview was later published in the July 12th edition of the *Sunday Mirror*. I have kept a copy of it as a souvenir of the day.

14

MY SOCIAL AND POLITICAL JOURNEY

ACTIVE POLITICS

I am a Bengali, and a Bengali without some political thinking and leaning is hard to find. In any case, the old state of Bengal (comprising West Bengal and East Bengal, now Bangladesh) had a long history of fighting for independence from British rule. It is not surprising that my interest in politics has its roots in Kolkata, one of the most politically minded cities in the world. While at the University, I was very much into Marxism and was a supporter of the Communist party of India (Marxist) despite the fact that Congress was the dominant party nationally and in most of the other states. The CPI (M) came into power in West Bengal in 1967, the year I came to the UK, and there was high hope that there would be dramatic improvement in the economy of the state and in the condition of the common people. Their rule initially lasted for six years, but subsequently they ruled

West Bengal in a dictatorial manner for about thirty-four years, from 1977 to 2011. The party lost popular support and suffered electoral defeat at the hands of the current ruling party Trinamool Congress at the general election of 2011. My support for the Marxist Communist party was very much dented as a result.

During my working life in the UK I did not have any active involvement in politics, mainly because the civil service code and standards of behaviour have always required civil servants to be politically neutral. However, as a socialist, my own personal political leaning was towards the Labour Party. After retirement, I did not want to sit idle and was keen get myself involved in serving the community, both locally and at national level. Very soon I became an active member of my local Residents Association at Canons Park (CAPRA) and also joined the Labour Party as a full member.

CANONS PARK RESIDENTS ASSOCIATION

My involvements with Canons Park Residents Association (CAPRA) made me familiar with many local issues and helped me to promote many initiatives in the interests of the Canons Park residents. Getting involved in work that is of benefit to local communities is a rewarding experience. For me, this was also a welcome starting point for an expansion of my interest and involvement in national issues.

It was a great honour for me to serve as the Chairperson for CAPRA for about six years, from 2006 to 2012. My link is still unbroken and currently I am the Association's Health Spokesman.

At a Fair with 3 other CAPRA Committee Members - Alan Davis,
Shirley Sackwild & the late Carlo Campioni

THE LABOUR PARTY

I joined my local Labour Group, Harrow East Constituency
Labour Party in 2010, which was the beginning of a journey
down a new road. I have since been its Political Education
Officer for a number of years. I was also privileged to serve as
the Vice Chair of the group for about two years. At the 2015
Labour Party leadership election, I strongly supported Jeremy
Corbyn despite strong opposition from many of my fellow
members. I had felt for a long time that the current Labour
leadership had lost its identity and were no longer in touch
with its working class roots. Jeremy Corbyn was a man of trust,
hope and principle who shared the concern of the common
people, the reason his subsequent election win was a landslide
victory. Sadly, we are living in a world of extreme violence,

conflict, and the threat of large scale wars. The need for people like Jeremy Corbyn, who believe and work for common good and peace for humanity, cannot be overemphasised. Whatever the future holds, I believe in what Mathew Parris, an eminent conservative journalist once said: *"You don't go into politics just to win but to win for something you believe in."*

EU REFERENDUM

More recently, the issue that has sharply divided this nation is one about the result of the EU referendum. To explain my

With London Mayor Sadiq Khan at a BBC Mayoral debate (2016)

personal view, I have always been a critic of the EU model and I was not alone. Michael Foot's commitment to leave the EEC is widely known. Tony Benn was a passionate internationalist, yet he very much disliked the EU. He denounced joining the Common Market as *"the most formal surrender of British sovereignty and parliamentary democracy that has ever occurred in our history."*

My opposition to the EU is mainly because of its undemocratic nature. It is run by an unelected executive, with a parliament that functions mainly as a rubber stamp. Economically, we should look at the real growth areas in Latin America and Asia. The result of the referendum – Brexit – has not yet been as cataclysmic as those who campaigned to "Remain" claimed it would be. Britain has simply opted to become like the countries in the rest of the world – USA, Canada, China, India and others.

INVOLVEMENT WITH OTHER ORGANISATIONS

My socio-political interests got me involved in a number of other organisations. Although there were several, I would like to make particular mention of the following three in the establishment or running of which I have taken an active role and ongoing interest.

SOUTH ASIAN FORUM (SAF) UK – This is an organisation formed to discuss and debate issues of concern to the South Asian community in the UK. I am a founder member of this organisation. The inaugural meeting was held in a committee room at the House of Commons on 12th June 2007, with three eminent speakers: Lord Meghnath Desai, the late Ashoke Kumar MP and Waqar Ahmed (pro Vice Chancellor, Middlesex University).

South Asians themselves are not a homogeneous group – there are deep divisions in terms of religion, language, culture, tradition, educational achievements and socio-economic status. Furthermore, as the South Asian community settled down in the UK and their families expanded to future generations, they are still faced with old issues of racism and cultural alienation, as well as the newly emerging issues of poor education, drug taking, crime, forced marriages, mental health, and religious fundamentalism. When we formed the SAF, what we had in mind was the need for an organisation to articulate these issues, raise awareness of them in an open-minded way and influence government thinking and policies on these issues. I have spent some valuable time as an active member.

NETAJI SUBHAS FOUNDATION (NSF) UK – This organisation was formed in 2002 with the twin objectives of promoting the ideas and vision of the revolutionary Indian leader Subhas Chandra Bose (Netaji), and to bring fairness in the attitude of the British Government towards him and his role during the Indian Independence Movement.

Very few people in this country have heard of Bose and for those few who are aware of him, he is a much maligned man because he sided with Germany and Japan to secure India's independence. Furthermore, there are many myths surrounding Netaji's death – much delayed declassification of the Government of India's secret documents have unearthed some truths, but not all. I and many other admirers of Netaji have held several events over the years to articulate Netaji's true image. He was not just a freedom fighter but a true statesman who, unlike most other contemporary national leaders, had a full vision and plan for India's future after independence. At one memorable event, we managed to persuade Netaji's daughter, Dr Anita Bose Pfaffs, who lives in Germany, to come and talk to us about her father as she knew him. The memories and thoughts she expressed about Netaji, and his work, were both captivating and poignant. I and the other NSF members were extremely happy that she chose to come to London and share them with us.

In another noteworthy event, the well-known journalist and historian, Anuj Dhar, came from India to London at our invitation. His extensive research and fight to bring out the truth about Netaji, led him to write a controversial book *India's Biggest Cover Up*, based on hard evidence from official records and interviews with many relevant personnel over many years. He gave a thought-provoking talk on his findings in this book, whose conclusions were substantially at variance with the official line about the supposed death of Netaji in a plane crash and his whereabouts after that.

Whatever the truth about Netaji's death, I and many other likeminded members of the NSF were, and still are proud of the work we are engaged in, to restore Netaji's true image– both in India and abroad.

LONDON KALIBARI

I have also been involved with another organisation called the London Kalibari. This is an association of the Indian Bengali community in London, established to promote various social, cultural and spiritual activities. Most of its events take place at a rental premises but the group is striving hard to acquire a permanent community centre.

It was the ex-Mayor of Harrow and current Treasurer of Kalibari, Mrinal Chaudhury, who familiarised me with the role London Kalibari plays in promoting the cause of the Bengali community. Since then, I have been privileged to be invited to speak on numerous special occasions. I was happy to talk about many socio-cultural subjects such as Asian Values, the Generation Gap, Humanity and Global Villages, Vivekananda and Tagore, Tagore and Nazrul, and Netaji Subhas Bose a National Leader.

One particular talk I gave couple of years ago attracted a great deal of attention and praise and also gave me an enormous amount of personal satisfaction. This was about Africa as part of Black History month celebrations in 2009. To be honest, I had a very little knowledge about African history before this celebratory event. I was, of course aware that Africa, a huge continent of more than 700 million people, was the "birthplace of the human race" dating from some 150,000 or so years ago. I was also aware that African history has been deliberately obscured and distorted by the legacy of colonialism. This, and the fact that there is a noticeable general apathy among many of us coming from the Indian sub-continent about Africa – whose colonial history in many respects is identical – prompted me to learn and talk about Africa's rich heritage. The success of this talk gave me a renewed enthusiasm to enhance my own knowledge about history in general and, more particularly, about Africa.

15

MY CULTURAL JOURNEY

GENERAL INTEREST IN CULTURE

I arrived in this country anticipating a nation full of people of culture familiar with Shelley, Keats, Bernard Shaw and other literary figures. What I observed in 60s and 70s was that while average middle-class people were generally well-informed, interested and enjoyed many cultural activities such as reading, theatre, museums, and sports such as cricket; the working classes' leisure time mainly involved bingo, cinema, greyhound racing and football. This is perhaps no longer true but in my view, there is still some difference between the so called "elite culture" of British people with higher education and the popular culture of common people who are caught up in their everyday lives.

In India, my main interest was in politics both academically and actively. My father was a well-known literary figure and a lifelong, ardent admirer of the internationally eminent Nobel Laureate poet and humanitarian, Rabindranath Tagore. I used

With British Politician Clare Short at a symposium in 2016.

to hear my father speak eloquently at many cultural events. As a Bengali, I also grew up in an environment in which reciting Tagore poems, Tagore songs or and listening to them was normal part of my culture This kindled in me some interest into the world of literature and arts including the life and work of Tagore but, I did not actively pursue this interest while growing up in India.

My interest in Tagore and Bengali culture gradually increased due to my close association with a well known literary person in Kolkata, the late Principal Shanti Sinha Ray, with whom I worked in Barrackpore College. I am immensely grateful to him and, also to the late Hiranmay Bhattacharya, the editor of a popular Bengali magazine *Sagar Pare* for his support and encouragement. Hiranmay Bhattacharya, who lived in East London, organised many socio-cultural events under the auspices of a well-known Kolkata-based Biswa Banga Sahitya Sammelon and he was kind enough to ask me to speak at many of these events. My cousin-sister Maya and brother-in-law Dr Shibabrata Biswas (himself a writer) have always encouraged and inspired me in the pursuit of my cultural life in London. My interest deepened when I came to know that the first reading of Tagore's monumental work *Gitanjali* took place in London and that two eminent British poets, William Rosenstein and W B Yeats, played a significant role in getting him nominated for the Nobel Prize, I actively started taking more interest.

THE TAGOREANS

In 1993 I welcomed the opportunity to join The Tagoreans, a London-based Bengali cultural organisation which, since 1965, has been seeking to promote Asian culture, literature, music and art with special reference to the life, work and ideals of Rabindranath Tagore. The invitation came from its Artistic Director, Mrs Gairika Gupta, wife of the late Tapan Gupta, the founder of this organisation. Because of his unexpected death, the organisation was going through a difficult period for some time. Gairika was persuasive enough to make me join the group. Since joining, I strove hard in various capacities both to revive and to raise the profile of the Tagoreans as a vibrant and forward looking cultural organisation whilst holding on to its rich tradition. I was pleased to be made the Treasurer and Vice Chair and then in 2003 I was honoured to be elected as the Chairperson.

The Tagoreans recently celebrated fifty years of success as a cultural organisation in London and I have had eighteen wonderful, enjoyable and productive years with them. I was fortunate to share a platform with many eminent literary figures including Lord Bhikhu Parekh, William Radice,

In front of Villa Miralrio where Tagore lived while in Argentina

Ketaki Kushari Dyson, Martin Kämpchen, Lord Meghnath Desai, the late Michael Marland, Satish Kumar, the late Prof Tapan Ray Chaudhury, Vincent Cable, Clare Short, at various literary events. During my time as Chair, the Tagoreans hosted numerous musical functions that included many eminent artists from Kolkata, including the late Maya Sen, Soumitra Chatterjee, Kaushik Sen, Rudraprsad Sengupta, Swatagalakhni Dasgupta, Pramita Mallick, Hemanti Shukla and others. They are too many events to narrate but as I reflect on them there are some anecdotes that come to mind.

The first of these concerns the legendary actor Soumitra Chatterjee (who starred in Satyajit Ray classic film *The World of Apu*), who was in London to present the much acclaimed play *Tiktiki,* in 1997. On the day of the event I took him in my car to the venue – Bharatiya Bidya Bhavan in West Kensington. Naturally, we talked about a lot of things in order to pass the time. When the conversation turned to sports he surprised me by his all-round knowledge across all forms of sports including cricket. However, then the journey took an awkward turn. While conversing, I missed an important turn and had to travel quite a distance before I could turn back and find the right road. Soumitra was not very amused as he wanted to reach the venue as early as possible. Luckily, not much time was lost in reaching the destination but for me, a fortuitous car journey with an eminent figure, which should have been thoroughly enjoyable, turned out to be quite embarrassing, although still full of interesting conversation! We later had several very enjoyable informal get-togethers with Soumitra, his talented co-star in the play Koushik Sen, his accomplished dancer wife, Reshmi, and the renowned Swapnasandhani group.

The other entertaining story worth mentioning concerns two eminent singers from Kolkata. When you want to listen to the voice of an artist of your choice, you will go to the musical venue where he or she is performing. If you can persuade the same artist to come and sing informally at your house, you consider yourself lucky. On a personal note, I was lucky on two different occasions.

The first occasion featured renowned Rabindrasangeet artist, Swagatalakshmi Dasgupta, who came to *London* at the invitation of The Tagoreans in 2003. Before meeting her, I was only aware of her through her unique rendition of the Tagore song *"He Nutan" (Hail – new dawn)*. I found her to be very warm and friendly and invited her one evening for an informal get-together at my house. She came and entertained us with some Tagore songs in her own inimitable style, without any accompaniment. One particular song she sang that evening at my request *"Ami roope tomaye bholabo na bhalobashaaye bholabo"* (*"I will not entice you with my beauty but win you with my love"*) was deeply touching for me and my wife.

The second occasion arose in 2005 when Nandikar, the

renowned drama group from Kolkata, came to present three plays. The Director of the group, Rudraprasad Sengupta was a university friend of mine and we had been very close since then. At one of our get-togethers at my home, Rudra was present along with other talented members of Nandikar including his wife, Swatilekha, their daughter Sohini, Goutam Halder and Debshankar Halder. While we were talking about one of my favourite Bengali songs from the film *Charulata*: *"Ami chini go chini tomere ogo bideshini" ("I know you, I know you well, O stranger, You lie across the seas")* Swatilekha sweetly started singing it using the only musical aid available at my house – a synthesiser. This wonderful gesture from Swatilekha and her lovely voice will always remain in my heart.

Among the many people who helped and encouraged me in my cultural journey, I would like to mention particularly the late Emeritus Professor Tapan Ray Chaudhury (Padmabhushan), the late Michael Marland (writer and educationist), Political Philosopher Lord Bhikhu Parekh (Padmabhushan), William Radice, (poet, scholar and Bengali

A Seminar with William Radice and late Tapan Ray Chaudhary,
late Syed Shamsul Huq and Ketaki Kushari Dyson

translator), Martin Kämpchen (creative writer and translator) and Valerie Doulton (writer, producer and director). I owe a great deal to each of them.

It is said "*Coming together is a beginning; keeping together is progress; working together is success*". The success of the Tagoreans during my years as Chair, was due to the kind help and support I received from Gairika Gupta, Manoshi Barua and other Committee members. In 2011, I decided to relinquish my role as Chair, partly because of other commitments and partly because I wanted to pass on this responsibility on to a younger member. The Tagoreans acknowledged my long contribution by making me their Honorary Adviser. I am pleased that the Tagoreans are continuing to be successful and there is now a strong group of young and energetic new members to carry on its good work.

INTEREST IN THEATRE

My cultural journey was not confined to the Tagoreans or for that matter literature. I had always been interested in theatre. My interest grew even more when I was studying in Kolkata. This city which, despite British actress Dame Janet Suzman's controversial assertion *that "theatre is a white invention"*, has a rich tradition of commercial and group theatres. My interest widened after coming into contact with Kolkata-based theatre group "The Nandikar" about whom I mentioned earlier. Part of my interest in theatre also goes back to one of my earlier memories in the 50s when I played a part in the formation of another renowned group "Sundaram" with the actor and director Manoj Mitra, film director, the late Parthapratim Chaudhury and the mime actor Jogesh Dutta among others on 15th August 1957. After coming to London, I participated in the production of two amateur Bengali theatres in London: *Jibanta Statue* at Manning Hall, University College London and *Sheheb Bibi Golam* at the Mermaid Theatre in London.

In London, where theatres enjoy enormous artistic reputation, I really enjoyed watching many wonderful productions. It is said that Britain lost an empire but has a global audience for its own popular culture in art, music, theatre and opera. At the opening ceremony of the last London Olympics, Danny Boyle presented this country as a country of singers, storytellers, actors and entertainers. I did not want to be a philistine and not make some effort to be familiar with the popular culture of this country.

Particularly memorable were *Phantom of the Opera* with Michael Crawford, Lillian Hellman's drama *The Little Foxes* with Elizabeth Taylor, *The Caine Mutiny Court Martial* with Charlton Heston and Ben Cross, *The Tempest* with Vanessa Redgrave and many others. The unique experience of seeing several Shakespeare plays being performed at the Globe Theatre on the South Bank, Regent's Park Open Air theatre as well as the Swan theatre in Stratford upon Avon are memorable. I never had much interest in ballet and opera but once I started watching them, my interest grew. It was an eye-opener for me to see two legendary ballet artists – Rudolf Nureyev and Margot Fonteyn performing together in *Sleeping Beauty*. Their perfect poise and graceful moves were wonderful to behold. Since then, I have had the good fortune to watch many popular ballets, such as *Swan Lake, Cinderella, Nutcracker* and *Giselle,* and thoroughly enjoyed them all.

LIKING FOR OPERA

I never thought I would ever come to like opera, with its

grandiosity of songs, emotions, costumes and orchestra. However, after watching some well-known operas like *Tosca*, *Aida*, and listening to great opera singers like Luciano Pavarotti, Placido Domingo, Jose Carreras and others, I discovered that operas could be an intense source of enjoyment, even for someone like me with very little knowledge of Italian, the most sung language in opera. Pavarotti's sonorous voice singing "*Nessun Dorma*" was, no doubt, one of the best I ever heard. This song itself has kindled interest in the minds of many who were not keen on opera.

16

SPORT IN THE UK

I have had a lifelong interest in sport. Not surprisingly, after arriving in London, I was keen to watch major sporting events in this country. In my bachelor days I was living in Maida Vale, which is close to the Lords Cricket ground. This gave me an ideal opportunity to watch many important test matches. After my marriage, I moved to Edgware in Middlesex. Middlesex no longer exists as a county but the name is used by the world renowned Marylebone Cricket Club (MCC)) whose home cricket ground is Lords – it's only half an hour by tube from where I now live, so there is no problem with me continuing to attend test matches there. This is also the reason why I took up membership of the Middlesex Cricket Club. Both for the fun of the experience and enjoyment. I worked as a steward for the MCC for a couple of years and enjoyed both working and savouring the unique atmosphere of Lords. Walking through the iconic Long Room inside the pavilion or sitting therein and watching cricket from there is an unforgettable experience.

INDIA AND THE CRICKET WORLD CUP

When India, as the underdog, won the Cricket World Cup (held in England in 1983) after beating the mighty West Indies in the final, I was present at the ground. Despite the "Tebbit test" of supporting the home country in cricket, the win gave me an enormous amount of pleasure and excitement. It was a very special day for me to remember always. My feeling about the Tebbit test in this respect is similar to what the well-known sports commentator, Matthew Syed, said about his Dad in a recent article in *The Times*, after Pakistan won the Champion's Trophy in 2017–

"My Dad can cheer Pakistan without loving Britain less."

After India won the Cricket World Cup, something more joyous unexpectedly followed, which I will always treasure in my heart. There was a need to keep the World Cup here

Holding the ICC World Cup with friend Kumar (1983)

in London in safe custody for a few days before it could be transported to India. A very close friend of mine, Kumar Senwalka, who had a family connection with the manager of the Indian Cricket Team at that time, volunteered to keep it. While the cup was in Kumar's house, he was generous enough to let me have the Cup in my keeping for three days. I have many photos of me, my son and daughter holding the World cup in our back garden. The memory of these three days will remain with me all my life.

PASSION FOR TENNIS

I have always had a passion for various sports. I enjoyed playing cricket, badminton and table tennis at club level both in India and in this country. My interest switched to tennis during my working life in the civil service. I was good enough to represent my Departments – the Department of Health and the Ministry of Defence – and as a team member in many inter-departmental competitions. I have been a member of my

Author (5th from left) with other ACORN LTC Members at a   Charity Tournament (2015)

local tennis club – Acorn LTC – for a number of years and love playing both competitive and social tennis there. There are many kind members, including the club chairman Stephen Phillips, who are volunteering their time to ensure that Acorn is a thriving, successful and sociable club. Not surprisingly, Wimbledon has been another of my favourite sporting arenas to visit. It is not easy to get tickets, but I have been lucky to get tickets either through my workplace or through my local tennis club for several important matches. I have seen many outstanding matches involving some of the greatest male and female tennis players of our times. To me the top three male players of all time are Rod Laver, Pete Sampras and Roger Federer. The best three female players I have seen are Martina Navratilova, Steffi Graf and Serena Williams. They have always provided memorable matches to the spectators at Wimbledon and other places.

LOVE FOR BRAZILIAN FOOTBALL

I love to attend football matches but mostly at international level. This was partly because in the 70s and 80s, racial problems were quite common on football terraces at club level. The problem is less acute nowadays but deep concerns remain over the appalling behaviour of some English fans on terraces abroad. The other reason is that for a long time I found the English league style of playing football defensive and negative. George Best was the most outstanding player I have seen in this country, but he played for Ireland. The import of some talented foreign players to the English league has now made it more exciting to watch. In football, I always loved to watch Brazil – to me, they are the best in the world. This is as much because of their remarkable record in the World Cup, as their naturally distinctive, fluid, attacking style of play which has always mesmerised football lovers throughout the world. To many, the Brazilian team of 1970 was the greatest football team ever assembled, with Pelé, Jairzinho, Tostao, Gerson, Rivelino and Torres, and others. It was a dream comes true for me to meet the legendary footballer, Pelé, personally and get a signed copy of his book *Pelé: The Autobiography* at one of his book launching events in London in May 2006.

In 2009 I went on holiday with my family to Brazil and Argentina. I was really keen to see the renowned Maracana football stadium in Rio de Janeiro. When I mentioned this to the manager of our hotel, he told me that all visits to the stadium were cancelled because of an important cup final match the following weekend between the two well-known Brazilian teams, Flamengo and Botafogo. I was deeply disappointed but my wish was fulfilled by a bizarre and unexpected stroke of luck. A family from the USA, staying in the same hotel, had bought four tickets for the above mentioned cup final match. Sadly, two members of their family were sick and the family decided to return their tickets. By a wonderful coincidence, I wanted four tickets for my family. So, when the manager offered them to me, I had no hesitation in buying them. With assistance from the manager, who organised transport, we were able to go to the stadium, see the match and return with an unforgettable experience.

ENGLAND AND MEDIA-DRIVEN HYPE

Although small in size and population, England has always been a truly sporting nation and has an admirable tradition of participating in all forms of sport and being successful. However, the commentators and media in general have shown a tendency to overrate England's achievements and underrate the quality and success of the other nations. England won the football World Cup over fifty years ago in 1966; in cricket they are yet to win the ICC World Cup. Yet what we regularly see, is the media-driven hype particularly in football, rugby and cricket that victory for England was there for the taking. There is now a gradual acceptance of the fact that this country no longer dominates sport and that there are other nations who can win more matches and tournaments. However, while the country's sporting importance in individual sports may have diminished, no other country, relative to its size, has contributed more to sport than the UK, and the breadth of this contribution was demonstrated through its strong performance in the last two Olympic Games. Furthermore, because of the current influx of British-born talented second and third generation Asians playing for England in football and cricket, the pendulum has swung towards Tebbit's test of supporting the home country by people of Asian origin. However, Moheen Ali, one of the most successful cricketers of Pakistani origin, must have detected some irony in it when he said *"People want me to do well and England to lose."*

17

CLASH OF CULTURES AND INTER-GENERATIONAL GAP

GENERATION GAP

We are familiar with George Orwell's observation: "*Each generation thinks itself to be more intelligent than the one that went before it and wiser than that comes after it.*" While this could be a simplistic statement, there is some truth in it. A recent finding that human intelligence is increasing by about three IQ points each decade due to improved health, education and nutrition, gives some scientific credence to this view.

The "generation gap" is common in many societies, but it is an issue that affects immigrant families in particular ways. When people are raised in different time periods, their perceptions, priorities and values about the world, can be quite different. This divide in understanding and interpretation between generations, gives rise to the so-called "generation gap". The on-going categorisation of different generations as Baby Boomers, Generation X, Generation Y, Generation Z, Millennials etc., is a reflection of this divide.

To immigrants in this country, the generation gap has an extra dimension. The issues facing first and subsequent Asian generations are in many respects different and complex, because they are being brought up within two vastly different cultures. As a result, they are finding it difficult to accept many of the traditional notions of the older generations of parents and grandparents. British journalist and author Sathnam Sanghera's *The Boy with the Topknot* tells us about his double life experience to reconcile the culture and traditional values of a Sikh family in Wolverhampton. Zaiba Malik's *We are a Muslim* depicts her life growing up in a Pakistani family in Bradford.

MY TALK AND OBSERVATIONS

I had the privilege of giving a talk on "Asian Values and Intergenerational Understanding" at some important venues in London, including the Nehru Centre – the cultural wing of the Indian High Commission. I was also interviewed in Broadcasting House (the London headquarters of the BBC) by Nihal, a well-known TV and Radio presenter of BBC *Asian Network Radio* on 1st April 2014. I spoke about the problems that Asians, growing up in this country, are facing, with Asian values sitting alongside western values, but in conflict with each other. The view I expressed was that many of the traditional notions of the Asian older generations, are increasingly being questioned and abandoned by the younger Asian generation. Priorities are taking a dramatic turn with regard to the importance given to the family, respect for parents, rights of the individual, value of education, love for material things, the role of women and other social and cultural norms. This is causing many undesirable consequences, including the break-up and a degree of unhappiness within Asian families.

If I have to identify one fundamental Asian value which gives rise to more controversy and resentment in its relevance and application to the younger Asians living in this country, it is the perceived lack of loyalty and respect towards parents and family. This is something most of the Asian parents find difficult to come to terms with. Consequently, the embracing of western influences in attitudes and tastes by their children is construed as making them rebellious and disrespectful. What adds to the anguish is the finding that their self-sacrifice is not inspiring similar behaviour in their children. In contrast, their children do not always have enough interest or adequate knowledge about their own parents' culture. This leads them very often to devalue the elderly and make jokes and comments about their lifestyle, accent, and behaviour. They also fail to recognise that the success of many young Asians in the UK, and globally – the "ethnic excellence" – is largely due to supportive families and their commitment and lifelong sacrifice.

However, to expect our children to do what our parents did for us or what we did for the children is both unrealistic and unreasonable. We forget that these are hard times for youngsters (both white and ethnic) with the additional burdens of growing up with the internet, student debt, the difficulty of finding work, the cost of housing and so on. The last thing the older generation should do, is to add to their despair and misery by trying to impose their own ideas and values. If our children fail to assimilate into larger British society it will be detrimental to their own well-being and success in life.

In this connection I read an article in *The Sunday Times* by Pravina Rudra of British Asian heritage, which I considered very insightful. She wrote about the peer pressure that she felt while growing up – to wear skimpy clothes, have boyfriends, and act and behave like a spoilt fun-loving teenager. The same pressure made her spend her adolescent life disregarding her parent's intelligence and benevolence. She expressed remorse about this later in life and said that many of her important lessons in life had come from her own heritage. This feeling was echoed by the actress Sunetra Sarker (who plays Dr Zee Hanna in *Casualty*) in a recent BBC documentary *Who Do You Think You Are,* shown on 22nd February 2017, after visiting India and Bangladesh to find out about her family's history.

Many years have passed since the arrival of the first generation migrants from the Indian subcontinent and East Africa. In the meantime, the UK has gradually accepted many positive social aspects of Asian values in the form of stable family life, discipline, good education, social festivities and the pursuit of peace of mind. On the other hand, the younger Asian generation is growing up valuing competition, admiring entrepreneurial skill, learning to be self-reliant because they know that to be successful in life, these are essential ingredients. Their embracing of many of the Western elements in the form of dress, music, language, and social behaviour, etc. is a sensible and practical way to become a part of the culture of that country, not necessarily an erosion of their own culture. This shows that neither the total disregard for Asian or Western values nor a blind allegiance to either will be of real benefit to the young Asians. Cultures do not enrich in isolation – they progress through intermixing – becoming cosmopolitan. If you imagine this country as an Olympic venue, *"Both old and young should carry the torch together."*

18

SOME TRAGEDIES

FAMILY TRAGEDIES

One aspect of living in both in India and England has taught me something important. I have learnt that loss is an inevitable part of life. While we grieve for our loved ones, we also need to celebrate their lives. I accepted losing my parents but losing my young nephew and sister-in-law unexpectedly was deeply upsetting. It challenged my own sense of security and confidence in the predictability of life.

The sudden death of my nephew Minku (Saugata) – Sumita and Sibesh's older son – at the age of just twenty-two, was a great shock and was met with disbelief. He had studied in London for about a year when Sibesh was here as a British Council Scholar. Minku was extraordinarily talented and brought immense pleasure to everyone who knew him for his sweet demeanour and gentle nature. We all miss Minku and his sudden death has left a gap in Sumita and Sibesh's lives which has been there ever since.

Their younger son Tubul (Shiladitya) has a successful career with Apple. He is happily married and settled in San Francisco with his wife Sweta and two beautiful children Tani and Sid.

My sister-in-law (my wife's sister) Benu, was beautiful, generous and a very caring paediatrician by profession. She came to London for a couple of years as a Nuffield Scholar to work at the famous Institute for Child Heath at Great Ormond Street Hospital. After the unexpected death of their father, Benu was the one who played the main supporting role in caring for the younger siblings. Furthermore, like my sister and brother-in-law, Benu also played an important part in bringing Gourie and me together in matrimony. Sadly she died prematurely at the age of forty-seven. Her death was a sad loss for everyone and we will miss her always.

More recently, my brother-in-law Asim Mukherji (Duluda) also passed away suddenly. He was a great source of strength and support to Gourie's family since my father-in-law passed away. He was a special person – caring, dutiful and amusing, who always brought humour and pleasure to everyone who knew him. I was lucky to have him as both as a family member and a close friend I will always remember.

LOSS OF CLOSE FRIENDS

Friends have always been an integral part of my life both in India and in the UK. While in India I had two very close friends from my school and college days. We were seen so often together, that many started calling us "The Three Musketeers". One was Indrajit Saha, a company director, whom I befriended during my University days. He was absolutely delightful company. The other was Debdas Pal, who was the Legal Secretary to the government of West Bengal at one time. Cultivated, thoughtful and like-minded, we were the best of friends for over fifty years. Sadly both have passed away. Ever since, I do not have any close friends in India except Manab Sarbadhikari, an Advocate of Kolkata High Court, who was also my good friend at University. I visit him regularly each time I go to Kolkata.

After arriving in this country, the first place I stayed in London was at a house in Huddleston Road near Tufnell Park which had a history of helping Indian newcomers. There was another house nearby on Anson Road, called Dr Sen's house, which had a longer history of putting up new arrivals from India and giving them lessons in British etiquette. Many Indian immigrants arriving in the 60s stayed in that house. At Huddleston Road, I made friends with another Bengali lodger, Gurudas Chatterjee, a very decent, honest and amiable man. My first initiation in cooking started under his tutelage. He had a reputation of being meticulous in everything including peeling and slicing onions and potatoes in a way that I admired but never mastered ! Our friendship continued for a number of years until his unexpected death in 1997.

Among all my close friends, Gurudas was the first among many to depart. His death was soon followed by the death of another lovable person with whom I became friends in London – Shantu Shome. He was a real gentleman, with a great sense of humour and loved to make merry quips. Sadly he died unexpectedly and we still miss him.

As mentioned earlier, I stayed at Huddleston Road for a few months and then moved to Randolph Avenue in Maida Vale to share a flat with a very close friend of mine, Pinu Shome. The flat had two other occupants Manthu Das and Deepak Ray and a frequent visitor Dipu Datta, all four of us coming from my own home town, Silchar. We had wonderful

Best man in close friend Pinu's wedding to Susan (1969)

times as friends both before and after getting married, having families and children. Dipu died more than a decade ago and then sadly Pinu and Manthu.

Dipu was very generous and warm hearted by nature. In the 60s, very few of my friends had their own cars. Dipu was the first to own a Triumph Herald and many times drove me round to visit places and meet up with friends. Manthu was an ideal flat mate. The flat was shared but he was happy to shoulder the bulk of the housework like shopping, cooking, paying bills. Manthu was a very good cook. If I had my intial training in cooking from Gurudas, my graduation would not have been complete without help from Manthu.

Pinu and I were friends for well over fifty-five years. We grew up in the same town of Silchar in Assam, played together, and went to the same school. He was the one who offered accommodation at 75 Randolph Avenue after my arrival in this country. The time we spent as friends since then is still vivid in my memory as our most enjoyable bachelor days, made even more wonderful by the presence of Susan, a young English girl from Kent with whom the very romantic Pinu was passionately in love. As we all expected, Pinu and Susan got married in 1969 and I was happy to be the best man at their wedding. Many a sweet reminiscence comes to mind of the times that Gourie and I spent together with Pinu and Susan over the years.

Reflecting on many other close friends that passed away I also have fond memories of Subroto Ghatak, with whom I forged an immediate rapport from my college days in Kolkata. We both came to this country in the same year. He was a natural academic – a university lecturer in Economics – and made a name for himself with several books and publications.

I recall an amusing incident at the time both Subroto and I were bachelors. I had a Morris Minor as my first car. One day I went to see him at his flat in Finsbury Park. We talked about all kinds of things during which he told me that he was learning to drive and asked me if he could to do some practice in my car for his forthcoming test. He assured me that he had already had several lessons and so I let him start the car with me sitting alongside and take it for a short spin. Subroto started the car but his foot slipped off the clutch and onto the accelerator. The car jumped the footpath and nearly hit a wooden fence in front of his flat. Luckily I was able to control the car, brought it back onto the road and no serious damage resulted. Subroto apologised for his carelessness. We both used to recall this incident quite often and laugh. Both my wife and I were in regular touch with him and his wife Anita throughout their working life in Leicester until his sudden death. Sadly, Anita also died at a relatively young age.

Along with the multiple losses of friends in a short period

of time, I also had difficulty in comforting some of my friends and close acquaintances who themselves had unexpected bereavements. I have many fond memories of them as loving husbands and wives. They will always be missed – never forgotten.

Aristophanes, the renowned comic writer of ancient Greece said *"Your lost friends are not dead, but gone before, advanced a stage or two upon that road which you must travel in the steps they trod."*

19

THE PROBLEM WITH OLD AGE

The social barriers created by inter-generational relationships are not the only problem older Asian adults face in this country. Another issue that is turning out to be problematic for the early migrants is coping with old age in this society. This was not something that we gave much thought to in our younger days. At the earlier stages of our lives, most of us were preoccupied with work during weekdays and socialising and having fun at the weekends. Life became hectic after marriage with the added responsibility of raising children, and planning their education. Time passed so quickly that there was no practical or mental preparation to face impending old age in this country.

Some first-generation immigrants firmly believed (or still believe) that they would go back to their own countries before they were too old. That turned out to be an illusion for many, partly because of the pain involved in being far away from their children and grandchildren and, partly because having spent so many years in England, we no longer have the same network of local support in India. Our contemporaries in

94

India are also getting old and we cannot depend on them to organise care when we require it. There is also the issue of the quality of medical care which we take for granted in this country. The problem is exacerbated by the death of either parent in a so-called nuclear family set-up in this country. In most cases, there is some bewilderment in the face of surviving family members, not knowing how to cope with the bereavement. Children and family friends stand in good stead in giving some comfort and support, but very soon either the husband or the wife have to face the harsh reality of a lonely life, particularly as their children have their own busy lives to live. In my experience, I found that the wives, in general, cope much better than the husbands with the loss – showing admirable resilience and toughness. This may be because, knowingly or unwillingly, most of the husbands were too dependent on their wives and were unable to show the same amount of toughness when faced with the sudden death of their spouses. This is an on-going problem now for most of the first generation immigrants in this country and the biggest fear is dying alone and no one finding out for days.

There is no simple answer as to how all of us will face up to the challenges of old age and death. Only time holds the answer to this question. Some internalise their feelings and cope with them alone; some fall apart for all to see; for some, with the support system they have, life gradually falls into places. Following an Indian philosophical teaching, one way of finding peace and happiness is to look at life at its different stages – the childhood and the student, the adult and married, the retirement and the ascetic. The ascetic stage for me is not that of renunciation but of living life to the fullest extent, appreciating all the people around me who have made me happy and contended. You only live once but if you have done your duties right, once is enough.

20

THE CHANGING FACE OF BRITAIN

INDO-BRITISH RELATIONSHIP

Despite their colonial history, there is something special and inexplicable in the relationship between Britain and India which began in 1600. That was the time Queen Elizabeth 1 granted a Royal Charter to the mighty East India Company to trade with India. After about 250 years, the company was wound up following the Indian mutiny of 1857. What is most interesting, however, is that although many attempts were made to revive the company, none were successful until an Indian businessman Sanjiv Mehta relaunched it in 2010 selling both prosaic and luxury brands of tea, coffee, chocolate and crockery from stores around the capital and abroad. What can be more ironic than this?

From an immigrant's point of view, I tried to trace the footsteps of "Peter", the first Indian to be officially recorded as arriving in England in 1614. Sadly no detailed record of Peter

At the Indian Forces Memorial in Ypres

has been found, except that the name Peter was given by King James 1. He was baptised at St Dionis Backchurch in the city of London and that at some stage he went back to India.

Nostalgia for the Raj still exists in the minds of both the British and Indians in my view. One would have expected from the Indians a lingering resentment towards their former colonial masters. Among many other historical facts not often mentioned, is that about one million Indians fought (of which 72,000 died) helping Britain in the First World War. The author and journalist, Sharbani Basu, has vividly described this in her book *For King and Another Country*. About a year ago, I visited the field near Ypres in Belgium where the fighting took place. I saw the Indian Forces Memorial near the Menin Gate and was immensely moved. The fact that the Indians, in general, bore no resentment towards their colonial rulers, speaks volumes about the ancient history of tolerance and the ability to absorb many different cultures that have flowed for thousands of years within their mother country.

There are many other enduring commonalities between the two countries: the use of English as a common language, parliamentary democracy, a professional civil service, a non-political army, an independent judiciary and so on. More people speak English in India than the sixty million people in Britain. India is also influencing the hearts and minds of the British through food, music, technology, Bollywood – the so called "soft powers". It is in keeping with this long and special relationship that the 70th anniversary of UK–Indian cultural ties is being celebrated throughout the year 2017.

MULTICULTURALISM

To those who came to the UK in the 60s or before, the changing face of Britain from the time when anti-immigration sentiments and 'Paki-bashing' were common, to what we see in the present day is vast and astonishing. One of the most popular musical TV programmes in the 70s was *The Black and White Minstrel Show* showing the blacking-up of the white people. This was accepted without demur at the time but the BBC had the good sense to axe it in 1978. Since then, over the years, we have witnessed the Government's response in the form of multiculturalism in the 80s and 90s as a vehicle to ensure respect for cultural diversity.

Multiculturalism as a concept has taken a battering in recent times. It is viewed by many as divisive, a barrier to integration, and encouraging of isolation and segregation in certain quarters. Sir Vidia Naipaul's assertion about immigrants ("*I want the country, I want the laws and the protection but want to live in my own way*") endorses this view. But this ignores the fact that institutional racism is a problem yet to be properly tackled. The ethnic minority are grossly underrepresented in most of the high powered professions. This has led many immigrants to live separate lives, socialise with their own kind only or rely on support systems only within their own communities.

Multiculturalism is of course, a "two-way street". Immigrants need to engage fully with the local community at all levels to ensure that they learn and respect the culture of the new country along with their own cultures. But for this to happen, discrimination and deprivation need to be tackled. Furthermore, the UK's white-dominated powerful institutions like the Judiciary, Police and Civil Service need to change to build respect between different cultural and social groups.

In this connection, I read an article by the Right Reverend Graham Tomlin, Bishop of Kensington recently, who raised another pertinent aspect of a multicultural society. According to him, *"The basis of a cohesive society is neither ethnic uniformity nor ethnic diversity for its own sake. It is compassion for those in need whatever their ethnic or social origin."* While one may detect religious overtone in what he said, one cannot disregard his strong conviction that *"The level of compassion for the defenceless is a barometer of the mental health of a society."*

Speaking about what constitutes "Indian-ness", the writer and politician Shashi Tharoor articulated some thoughts which are pertinent to multiculturalism: *"If America is a melting pot then to me India is a thali, a selection of sumptuous dishes in different bowls. Each tastes different, and does not necessarily mix with the rest, but they belong together on the same plate, and they complement each other in making the meal a most satisfying repast."* This means that, in a multicultural society, people should be free to preserve their roots but also to live amicably without interfering in each other's cultures so that society is both multi-flavoured and enriched by hybridity. Such a society empowers and benefits everyone.

These aspirations are neither unreasonable nor indeed unachievable in today's Britain. What was unthinkable not so long ago is now happening: the Indian festival of Diwali is celebrated in Trafalgar Square and (more unbelievably) at 10 Downing Street. As Emma Duncan, the deputy editor of the *Economist* said in *The Times, "Today's Britain is a nicer place than yesterday's. Tomorrow's will probably be better still"*

21

CONCLUSION

HOME IS BOTH INVISIBLE AND PORTABLE

As I look back on my life in two parts – in India and in England, with both parts gradually merging into one, I am astonished by the way it unfolded and progressed. My astonishment is because, while living in India, I never visualised that I would ever make England my permanent home. I was fortunate to be born in a country enormously rich and diverse in its history with an ancient culture of tolerance and reciprocity. My migration, both by chance and good luck, happened to be to a country with a distinct Anglo Saxon identity, but, as Michael Portillo said *"everyone is a bloody foreigner somewhere"*. It is also a country where historically many foreigners have been beneficiaries of its generosity. I have been fortunate to have two different experiences to draw upon and, being enriched by both, to blend in and contribute to British life in a range of fields.

Over the last fifty years, I found numerous like-minded

people both at work and in my social life. I had some amazing colleagues at various stages of my career within the Department of Health and the Ministry of Defence. My heart is filled with many wonderful memories of my interaction with them. More particularly, the personal friendships that have grown up out my contact with some of them, in particular with John Arnold and Maurice May from the MOD; David Burns and Mike Preston from DOH, have become an important part of my life. I stay in contact with them via email and also meet up for a meal and drinks very often.

Socially, I shared beliefs and commitments to many good causes and strived towards achieving them. By expounding on the importance of promoting good community relations, I feel I have made some useful contribution towards social cohesion between the immigrants and the general British public, particularly at local level. According to D.J.W. Strumpfer, a Professor of Psychology from South Africa, *"Our strengths in life come and grow out of hard endeavour, experience, personal learning, and loving relationships with other people and connection with the community"*.

A recent nationwide survey titled "Bittersweet Success" by the Policy Exchange think tank, applauded the immigrants in their fulfilment of the *"immigrant promise – hardship today for the implicit promise that tomorrow will be brighter for the kids"*. Both my wife and I strove hard to have a happy and fulfilling family life. Each time I visit India, I return with wonderful memories of time together with our brothers, sisters and their families. All in all, I feel I am more relaxed in myself in my old age. It is time for me to cherish my yesterdays, live happily my today's and not be fearful about my tomorrows.

Nobel Laureate Economist Amartya Sen, in his book, *Identity and Violence*, stressed the fact that identities are robustly plural, therefore, I could be a Bengali, an Indian, a Hindu, and British. Any one of these identities need not or should not obliterate the others. You learn and benefit from various identities.

As regards home, Pico Iyer, the celebrated British born essayist and novelist of Indian origin said correctly in my view, *"My home is both invisible and portable."* Fugitive Writer Taslima Nasrin's life has been one of constant move from one safe home to another. *"My home is in the hearts of the people who believe in me."* she said. Following Mark Tully, the celebrated British Journalist and BBC India correspondent, *"your native place is where you feel at home, not necessarily where you were born"*. There is also the practical argument that, in these days of globalisation and easy travel, you should be prepared to pull up your roots and establish a new native place.

For my final thoughts on home and identity, I can do no better than quote the great humanist poet, Rabindranath Tagore. In one of his many memorable poems in Gitanjali (*Collected poems and Plays, published by Macmillan*), he said:

"Thou hast made me known to friends whom I knew not,
Thou hast given me seats in homes not my own,
Thou hast brought the distant near and made a brother of the
　　stranger.
I am uneasy at heart when I have to leave my accustomed shelter:
I forget that there abides the old in the new, and that there also thou
　　abides.
Through birth and death, in this world or in others, wherever
　　thou leadest me it is thou, the same, the one companion of my
　　endless life whoever linkest my heart with bonds of joy to the
　　unfamiliar.
When one knows thee, alien there is none, then no door is shut."

The Bengali version of it:

"*Koto ojanerey janailey toomi, Koto ghorey diley ttie,,*
Doorke koreeley neekot, bondhu Porke koreele bhai.........."

is widely known to all Bengalis.

All I can say is that I have believed in this ethos throughout my life and I still believe firmly in it.

The celebrated author Rudyard Kipling famously said "*The East is East and West is West, and never the twain shall meet*". Well, the twain have met – in me and in many other immigrants and their descendants living in this country as British Asians.

REFERENCES

Introduction

Ed Victor The Times Obituaries 9 June 2017

Chapter 1

Sumita Bhattacharya "My Dad" 1977
Silchar- Wikipedia

Chapter 2

BBC News South Asia   "Court Changes Calcutta's History"   16
    May 2003
Adam Hopkins -"Giving crazy Calcutta a chance" The Times Travel
    28 November 1998.
 "Job Charnock is not Kolkata founder; Kolkata High Court" –
http://kamdev.faithweb.com.
Encyclopaedia Britannica – Indian History "Black Hole of Calcutta"
The Straight Dope Report- "Is the Black hole of Calcutta a myth" 9
    October 2001

J Thakerar - 'Anglo-Indians' - A Talk by an army veteran as posted on 17 September 2016

Chapter 3
_____

History of Barrackpore http://barracpore.westbengal.online.in/city-guide.

Chapter 4
_____

Harry Mount - "Water wind and wet weather make us British" The Times, 6 June 2012

Clare Foges - "Raise a glass to saving the great British pub" The Times, 15 February 2017

Editorial - "Rise of the Micro pubs" The Times, 23 November 2015

Chapter 5
_____

Peter Brookes – "Summer of Love - It was a truly golden fabulous time" The Times, 3 June 2017

"Hair Musical http://hairthemusical.com.

David Sanderson "V&A offers a trip down memory lane" the Times, 27 February 2016

Chapter 7
_____

Wikipedia "Haileybury and Imperial Service College"

Sukhdev Sandhu – Tagore Memorial Lecture"England through Indian eyes" Royal Society Lecture 2010

Phillip Aldrick- "Smallest civil service since 1939 as austerity cuts bite" The Times 17 September 2015

David Budworth "The truth about public sector pensions" The Times, 25 June 2011

Chapter 8

Pravina Rudra "Finding out my parents had had an arranged marriage was like finding out that Santa Clause was not real" Cosmopolitan, 8 September 2014

Chapter 10

Anthony Heath and Sheila Jacobs "Comprehensive Reform in Britain" 1 June 1998 www.crest.ox.ac.uk/papers.htm.

Greg Hurst "Ofsted Chief Attacks 60s throwbacks" The Times, 21 June 2014

Jenni Russel review of "The Triple Package" by Amy Chua and Jed Rubenfeld, The Sunday Times Books 9 February 2014

Chapter 12

Nicola Twilley "The Last Places" 24 January 2013 http://ediblegeography.com.

Sujit Bhattacharjee "Reflections of a Retired Ethnic Minority Steering Committee Member" Paper Clips MOD issue 124 May 1999

General Lord Dannatt "Do we really want a politically correct British Army" - extract from his book "Boots on the Ground" The Times 1 October 2016

Chapter 13

"Her majesty requests the pleasure- Royal Garden Party" Sunday Mirror, 12 July 1998

Chapter 15

Nadeem Badshah article on Dame Janet Suzman's claim that "Theatre not in culture of other races "The Times 9 December 2014

Chapter 16

Simon Barnes "Why thinking of England reflects new reality" The Times 28 May 2012
Richard Hobson "People want me to do well and England to lose" The Times 2 August 2016
Simon Barnes "Wisden debate is all over bar the shouting" The Times
22 April 2011
Matthew Syed "My dad can cheer Pakistan without loving Britain less" The Times 21 June 2017

Chapter 17

Pravina Rudra "SO, WHERE ARE YOU FROM" The Sunday Times 17 July 2016
Nihal BBC Asian Network Programme 1 April 2014

Chapter 19

Oriental philosophy "Hinduism: the four stages of life" www. philosophy.lander.edu.

Chapter 20

Indo British Heritage Trust 400 Press Release "A defining moment in Indo –British relations" December 2015

James Hurley "Rebirth of trader that unified global lifestyle" The Times, 14 July 2014

Adam Fresco "With one eye firmly on the past, new chapter begins for East India Company" The Times 8 February 2010

Emma Duncan "Believe it or not, the bigots are dying out" The Times, 28 October 2014

The Right Rev Graham Tomlin "Think carefully before joining the backlash on migrants" The Times Credo 30 January 2016

John Elliott "Naipaul lashes out at 'multi-culti' Britain" The Times, 5 September 2004

Shashi Tharoor "Indian Identity is forged in diversity. Every one of us is in a minority" The Guardian 15 August 2007

Melissa van der Klugt "Chapattis and Hookahs in the trenches" - review of Shrabani Basu's book 'For King and Another Country' the Times 26 November 2015

Rosemary Bennett "Racial integration is a two way street" The Times, 8 February 2011

Chapter 21

Amartya Sen "Identity and Violence –the illusion of destiny"

Michael Portillo "Remember, everyone is a 'bloody foreigner' somewhere" The Sunday Times, 18 April 2004

Mark Tully "Rooting For Home" Outlook 2009

Pico Iyer "Where is Home" http://en.wikipedia.org/wiki/Pico_Iyer

UK Indians lead in education, business success – 13 November 2016
https://www.easterneye.eu/uk-indians-lead-education-business-success/

Rabindranath Tagore Gitanjali (Song Offerings) Verse 63 Visva –Bharati UBSPD